SWITCHING

BILLION-DOLLAR

CONVERSATION LINES

Family Offices and Multi-Generational Success

Anne Klein • Brian DeLucia

SWITCHING

BILLION-DOLLAR

CONVERSATION LINES

Family Offices and Multi-Generational Success

From dialing code +212,
New York City, United States of America

to +27, Pretoria,
South Africa,
and the international arena – dial +X

@ 2024 Brian J DeLucia & A.M.M Klein

Contact details:

Switchingconversations@outlook.com

ISBN: 978-1-0370-0124-6 (print)   978-1-0370-0125-3 (e-book)

Anne has intentionally taken steps to educate her children about family assets, the meaning of family wealth, her position on fair treatment, and the contributions of each family member.

> This book is dedicated to
> Anne's wonderful children,
> Janecko and Zhanna.

ABOUT THE AUTHORS

In the generational landscape,
enthusiasm is our driving force.

anne Klein   *Brian DeLucia*

The authors of *Switching Billion-Dollar Conversation Lines, Family Offices & Multi-Generational Success* were introduced before the 2020 lockdowns.

Despite facing various professional, personal, and business barriers, they are keenly interested in family offices, founder-led companies, intergenerational planning, and creating opportunities for others.

Brian and Anne recognize that differences and challenges often lead to innovation and unity through **shared values**, leading to a greater purpose, similar to the history of successful families.

They created this book to share the knowledge and wisdom that they gained with the international family office community and the generational wealth profession — particularly in areas that are often a mystery to others.

Their single and shared experiences as well as their practical insights made it possible to author this useful and meaningful work.

To our Family, Friends, Industry Members, and the Families we serve ...

If you can give your child only one gift, let it be enthusiasm.

Bruce Barton

Brian DeLucia is a respected family office influencer who specializes in real estate, critical infrastructure, and old economy recurring revenue businesses.

His unique ecosystem of resources and experiences combines other family offices, institutional capital, and real-world scenarios to build strategic relationships within the confidentiality framework.

Aligning shared goals with missions and values is an important dynamic in Brian's daily approach to life.

He communicates regularly with attorneys, accountants, advisors, family offices, and asset owners to gather and *share* intelligence.

Additionally, Brian embodies a disciplined philosophy of family governance that aligns with its mission and values to uphold risk management, health, safety, and security of its members. Brian ensures that his family legacy in the real estate industry lives on through his participation in events and conversations. His love for competitive sports demonstrates his desire to thrive in a competitive industry.

www.arrrivatollc.com

Anne Klein is a second-generation lawyer with years of experience in the private advisory, *multi- and single-family office* industry.

She's a South African attorney, notary, and conveyancer who works with influential families, business owners, executives, and stakeholder networks.

Anne is a member of professional societies, enthusiastic about family philanthropy and governance, and has served as a fiduciary and advisor to successful families.

She holds a QFOP certification from the *Family Office Club in the United States of America* and founded a private office to support family offices and the transfer of generational wealth.

Anne has received various industry accolades and was a cameo contributor to *The Practical Guide for Wealthy Families and Family Offices* by Paul Roper, Nicky Dewar, and Ian Murphy.

www.luciadk.com

Knowledge is more valuable than gold,

and sharing it increases its intrinsic value.

The book's authors are eager to learn from others and are pleased to share their knowledge. Because they are willing to learn from others, *they create space for readers to capture their thoughts and take inspired action.*

This work encourages and allows for active participation by, you, the reader. The authors would love to hear your thoughts as you engage with the different topics covered. They look forward to receiving your feedback on your insights and even opposing thoughts, should you have any.

Anne and Brian understand that sharing knowledge is crucial in creating a cohesive environment for everyone involved in the stakeholder network. The authors prefer to teach rather than lecture and to gain wisdom through conversations and action.

They are well-versed and experienced industry participants. They enjoy participating in local and international institutional conferences and networks. With their decades of industry experience, they have gained access to exclusive conversations and practical knowledge. They intend to share their expertise and insights in this work.

The intention is to transform families' and advisors' perspectives and ideologies that might sometimes rock the boat. It includes technical concepts, practical support, and ideas on self-improvement because each life counts. The book aims to showcase family offices' inner workings and empower the stakeholder networks with other ideas as well as areas of concern.

The framework

Unlike most other financial-oriented publications, this work was designed to allow readers to generate ideas for their families, businesses, and professions by actively reflecting on a legacy plan *while reading*, realizing that specific unspoken topics are needed to be addressed to create stronger families.

It provides an excellent framework for making complex decisions in challenging and favorable times; it enables one to understand that there are quick access points to opportunities when they arise.

Acknowledgments

The authors express their gratitude to the professionals in their network. They understand that the professionals in the *family office community* often work independently due to the nature of their work. However, they believe that sharing knowledge within the community can enhance the quality of solutions and support a more comprehensive network.

Family office professionals are interdependent, and this book is a collection of influential minds that have helped shape its content over many years.

The authors are thankful for the support they have received over the years. Their views on the world, particularly the *family office world*, have evolved and continue to shift.

This publication *Switching Billion-Dollar Conversation Lines, Family Offices and Multi-Generational Success* flows from the combined knowledge pool of various professionals and families with whom the authors engaged over many years. The authors gained valuable insights during their contributions to the community.

This work was made possible with invaluable informal guidance and solid crafting. While the authors cannot extend their appreciation to all who informally contributed to its creation, they would like to express their gratitude to those who invested their time and effort to provide insights and resources over the years.

Their invaluable contribution enabled them to produce this book, and they are profoundly grateful for the industry's unwavering support.

Based on the principles of trust, confidentiality, and integrity, the information is shared to level the playing field between different role-players.

LDK — A — LDK

The authors' wish

Be yourself; everyone else is taken.

Oscar Wilde

The power of three wishes

The authors have three wishes for their readers. They hope everyone who reads it will take away at least three crucial things with them:

♦   The importance of working in alignment.

♦   To improve their own understanding of the industry.

♦   To share their wisdom and knowledge to create better solutions and take inspired and trustworthy action for a better world.

The authors are firm believers that each family, regardless of the level of wealth, must empower themselves through knowledge, to build a stronger future for humanity.

The Wealth Switch – Allows For The Switching Of The Guards

Don't miss the switch because of lack of participation!

Let's Talk!

#NX-GEN Success

and

#NX-9-12$zeros Family Offices

Anne Klein   Brian DeLucia

Content

Foreword

I am happy to present *Switching Billion-Dollar Conversation Lines, Family Offices and Multi-Generational Success* — an unusual approach to the subject matter.

This book clearly culminates rigorous research, practical experience, and deep industry insights. It represents influential families and offers authoritative analysis, ensuring you are well-informed and confident in the information presented.

The book is a collaborative effort by two individuals from diverse geographical, cultural, and professional backgrounds, ensuring a comprehensive and balanced perspective on topics they both respect.

While some views may be more aligned with a specific area of expertise or jurisdiction, the aim is to provide you with a global understanding to help you create awareness, find clarity, take steps, and find balance.

Above all, this book results from constructive collaboration between the authors. They are always seeking to improve their outlook and welcome your thoughts. In conclusion, I hope you enjoy the book and its fresh insights.

The authors suggest that authentic multi-generational wealth is established through family office structures, independent of the definition ascribed to the term *"Family Office."*

It is obvious that they have deliberately refrained from delineating distinct boundaries between various themes and definitions, asserting that optimal solutions are those tailored to meet a family's specific circumstances, long-term objectives, and strategies at any given time and place.

This guide and workbook *(the book)* provide genuine insights into unfamiliar worlds, drawing on diverse perspectives from South Africa to the United States and beyond. They equip readers with tools to develop their *multi-generational plans*.

While not all families need a family office, families need to have a *Family Governance Plan* as a starting point for generational success, and this guide assists with that journey.

Both Anne and Brian's philosophies underpin this work and the fact that they unhesitatingly approach difficult issues in a straightforward manner will no doubt make for lively debates.

Perhaps a Family Office conversation starter is
as simple as beginning with Hello.
Brian DeLucia

Each generation counts and keeps score;
make your generation one for the scoreboard.
Anne Klein

It is my opinion that anybody involved with family offices or who act in any form of advisory capacity in the wealth industry, would benefit from not only reading this book but also from participating in the journey that is outlined between the covers.

Having worked in the industry's business, technical, and practical sides, they understand the importance of taking a holistic view of the families they have engaged with, the industry participants, and the professionals they learn from and with whom they engage.

Thomas R. Brigandi

Thomas R. Brigandi Foundation

www.brigandifoundation.org

LDK — A — LDK

Let's Share ...

In the spirit of this book's intention, we, the authors, would like to ease you into our first sharing opportunity before we journey into the depths of this guide.

Impossible is the word found only in a fool's dictionary.
Wise people create opportunities for themselves
and make everything possible...
Napoleon Bonaparte

SWITCHING
BILLION-DOLLAR
CONVERSATION LINES
Family Offices and Multi-Generational Success

Our Take ...

Family offices have a distinctive approach to finding opportunities in uncertain times. They do so by engaging in genuine conversations with key players.

Family offices prioritize long-term success and secure it through strategic engagement with stakeholders who share their goals, creating *generational strategies.*

Families and businesses require structure and strategy to create meaning, even in a borderless world. Now is the time to reflect and act towards sustainable wealth stories.

In times of hardship like wars and pandemics, multi-generational family businesses have survived by adapting to change and navigating transitions. However, as generations move forward, the closeness between family members often diminishes. Thoughtful planning and a team of aligned advisors who share the family vision can significantly increase the likelihood of success.

Fledgling entrepreneurs approaching family offices often need to pay more attention to the fact that family offices are not inexperienced investors. Most investors who invest millions into a business have earned millions in that sector. Work with the families, provide solid options, and embrace the family culture.

Your Take ...

My name:

My family name:

Date:

My take on success:

My wishes:

My switch:

The Book in Context

Anticipated wealth transfers, amounting to trillions of dollars over the next two to three decades, underscore the critical need for robust multi-generational planning, asset protection, effective family governance and philanthropy practices.

Families are becoming global and mobile and are abandoning traditional ways of doing things.

In addition it has become more difficult to identify a family leader when the **wealth creator** is no longer around, and proactive planning fails.

Consequently, the number of family offices internationally is continuing to rise rapidly, creating an increasing demand for superior guidance, services, and wisdom. Navigating the world of **family offices** is a complex and dynamic journey that can give rise to a disconnect between the family's world and the world of different role-players, especially when it comes to generational transfers of wealth. A substantial number of family offices simply fail, often due to insufficient sensitivity to the human element and its related challenges.

The scarcity of advisors, compounded by an aging advisory cohort and restricted access to exclusive forums, have resulted in numerous untold narratives and unexplored scenarios.

Wealthy clients and family office advisors tell us that the aforementioned tend to give rise to numerous problems that can negatively impact the family office, the generational wealth story, and the family world. They also stated that women will play a significant role in the great transfer of wealth, yet their roles within family offices are not always clearly defined.

They highlighted issues such as:

♦ The lack of understanding of one another's terrain often results in friction impacting the family office's performance. This results in:

⇒ *An inability to take decisive action within a rapidly changing landscape.*

⇒ *Limited access to opportunities and the freedom to choose.*

♦ Difficulty in identifying an effective family leader when the original wealth creator is no longer around. A serious number of widows continue to express their regret that they had not taken a keener interest in securing and growing their family's financial future. Consequently, they fear what would happen to the sustainability of wealth over future generations.

This factor is further exacerbated by the generational gap — in terms of values, experience, skills, and knowledge — which becomes very visible in the absence of the original wealth creator. Naturally, this factor has its ramifications, such as:

⇒ *Not fully understanding the need for robust family governance structures and how crucial it is to protect the family's legacy.*

⇒ *Evaluating and appointing effective and trustworthy advisors can be a daunting task to the uninitiated. Choosing the wrong successors without going through a formal process can destroy the family legacy and chase away good advisors.*

♦ Discovering changing regulations too late impacting on maintaining meticulous records, which leads to the family being vulnerable in terms of:

⇒ *Protecting the family's privacy and legacy.*

⇒ *Navigating intricate business dynamics.*

⇒ *Dealing with the scattered nature of available knowledge.*

We must not overlook the potential consequences of not having access to the correct information and people: financial loss, strained relationships, wasted time, damage to reputation, and other risks.

Wealthy family members and advisors also confirmed that:

♦ Family offices need to have advisors who are sensitive to the current and future needs of the family.

♦ Being proactive, staying ahead of the curve, and making well-informed decisions are critical for the success of a family office.

♦ Establishing a robust family governance structure is crucial to preserving family stories and protecting the future of the family legacy, particularly given the constantly evolving nature of businesses.

Through further discussions, it became apparent that if the above concerns could be addressed effectively, it would:

♦ Create better opportunities and solutions when families and advisors align their knowledge and skills.

♦ Enhance the opportunities to keep the family story intact should there be pro-active legacy planning.

♦ Assist legacy families in taking the lead when it comes to people, relationships and issues confronting humanity.

♦ Provide wisdom that assists where knowledge fails, and access to wisdom requires time and resources.

♦ Address the unique story of each as the generational stories can improve through the art of active participation and planning.

All of the aforementioned gave rise to this book. So, let's help the **BILLION-DOLLAR SWITCH** to **CREATE THE SWITCH** for a better tomorrow. Just to reiterate ... *Wisdom* assists where knowledge fails, and access to wisdom requires *time and resources.*

> *Men often oppose a thing merely because*
> *they have had no agency in planning it or because*
> *it may have been planned by those whom they dislike.*
>
> Alexander Hamilton

Family Offices ...

Where the word impossible is seldom an option or an answer.

Multi-generational success ...

Means empowering yourself and others with wisdom and taking inspired action to achieve something impossible for the logical mind.

Starting a family office doesn't require a grand entrance or formal announcement. To succeed, focus on fulfilling specific criteria and presenting numbers and results, showcase expertise, and have engaging multi-generational success stories are about families who have taken intentional actions to create an environment where every family member has a voice, where the collective vision is more important than any one individual, where there are shared values, and where uncomfortable challenges and truths are not ignored but acknowledged and addressed.

The Wealth Switch – *Allowing for the Switching of the Guards*

Don't miss the switch because of your lack of participation. Now is a good time to empower yourself.

The estimates

The estimates regarding transferring wealth to heirs, charities, taxes, and estate closing costs keep changing like the landscape.

Different reports have various estimates, but US$59 - US$82 trillion or more could be transferred. It has been said that if the growth rate is two percent, charitable giving could reach up to US$27 trillion; if it reaches three percent, it could exceed US$40 trillion. Furthermore, within the next 20 to 30 years, over 1,000 billionaires are expected to transfer more than US$5 trillion to their children.

A 5% wealth tax on multi-millionaires and billionaires in the G20 could generate US$1.5 trillion annually. Taxes keep changing and a good tax advisor would be necessary to unpack the relevant complexities. (Please note that the figures quoted are based on a variety of available resources.)

Generational transition

This generational transition has already begun and brings new ideas about business, investment, and philanthropy. Family wealth will take on different forms based on the family's multi-generational planning, the demise of the patriarch or matriarch, asset consolidation, business strategies, and philanthropy. Family philanthropy is crucial for the most successful families to have a sustainable future, even if there might be different ideas and ideologies from individuals, businesses, and family members.

Inherited wealth versus earned wealth, what's the difference?

Inherited wealth and wealth earned and created require different approaches and treatments from individuals. A trend suggests that inherited wealth may be less likely to be donated to charitable organizations once the new recipient has received it.

Families should address structured and planned philanthropy as part of their generational story, as unstructured giving can lead to undesirable outcomes.

Advisors must be mindful of how wealth was accumulated and created to understand the family's needs and outlook fully. Conversely, families must capture their family story to make it more impactful for generational discussions and create a switch.

YOUR switch ...

Learn more about Family Offices and generational success strategies. This exciting and curious world will rapidly change your wealth journey. The time is now; don't be left behind by the new wave of wealth creators. Your family and business associates will thank you for being ahead of the curve. Be the one to make the switch.

OUR switch ...

1,000 Billionaires Begin $5,200,000,000,000 Transfer of Wealth –

And the 'Heirs To Billionaires' Have Their Ambitions.

The Daily Hodl

Inside the billionaire landscape

The Great Wealth Transfer, where the conversations include the numbers.

Timeframe

While the transfer of wealth among the world's super-rich is rapidly increasing, it's already impacting the heirs of billionaires, who are gaining more prominence and wealth than ever.

Interestingly, we need to find new ways of serving families; new billionaires receive more inheritance than they acquire through entrepreneurship, a significant shift from previous trends.

This shift is noteworthy because these heirs have diverse views on business, investment, and philanthropy, shaping the current business landscape. They are keenly aware of their challenges, including pandemics, climate change, geopolitical tensions, and war. They are aligning their wealth toward new business opportunities that can address these issues.

We show you the way

Billionaires are looking for ways to invest their wealth to help them navigate these challenges and achieve long-term sustainable outcomes. They are increasingly interested in impact investing, where they can manage businesses that benefit society and the environment and provide commercial returns.

This approach reflects a shift towards delivering sustainable outcomes across all activities rather than just classic grant-giving philanthropy.

Zeros add more power

Billionaire heirs are crucial in shaping the world's future. They have the power to drive equitable technological and environmental transformation for all. There are currently just over 2,500 billionaires worldwide, 1,023 of whom are aged 70 or older.

Self-evaluations

There are times when we all require some self reflection, regardless of wealth. However, this becomes a very critical component for family offices and their advisors.

For this reason we have included a few self-evaluation questionnaires to stimulate some thinking around the subject of the mindset of billionaires and their advisors.

Honest answers would make the evaluation more meaningful and it can be a useful tool for development and future strategies.

The maximum score for the Billionaire Mindset is 70. In our experience, it is unlikely that every family member would score 70.

The same would be true for advisors. The maximum score for the mindset of an authentic advisor is 65 and for advisory teams the maximum score is 40.

The leader is one who, out of the clutter, brings simplicity...

out of discord, harmony... and out of difficulty, opportunity.

Albert Einstein

The Billionaire Mindset

If you are a billionaire, or if you are supporting billionaires, you would benefit from exploring the following qualities. Evaluate the extent to which you agree with each statement on a scale of 1 to 5. / 1= I don't agree — 5 = I totally agree.

1. Billionaires understand that intelligence and abilities can be developed.　① ② ③ ④ ⑤

2. They recognize there is an abundance of opportunities to acquire wealth by fostering a positive attitude towards money.　① ② ③ ④ ⑤

3. They possess a strong sense of purpose and unwavering confidence in achieving their goals.　① ② ③ ④ ⑤

4. They believe that consistent and focused action yields a cumulative impact and that celebrating small victories motivates them to pursue larger aspirations.　① ② ③ ④ ⑤

5. Billionaires embrace challenges and overcome fears, which are pathways to personal growth and success.　① ② ③ ④ ⑤

6. They value healthy competition as a means of self-improvement in a world where mediocrity prevails.　① ② ③ ④ ⑤

7. Time is regarded as their most valuable asset, and they are unafraid to take calculated risks.　① ② ③ ④ ⑤

8. They view failure as a stepping-stone to progress.　① ② ③ ④ ⑤

9. Setting clear goals, prioritizing personal development, and cultivating multiple income streams are essential.　① ② ③ ④ ⑤

10. Visualization, accountability, and continuous learning are integral to their mindset.　① ② ③ ④ ⑤

11. They strive to live within their means, prioritize discipline and adaptability, and remain focused amidst distractions.　① ② ③ ④ ⑤

12. Additionally, they are committed to identifying and addressing their mental and physical weaknesses.　① ② ③ ④ ⑤

13. Financial stability gives them a sense of freedom.　① ② ③ ④ ⑤

14. Lastly, they believe that acquiring wealth should be a means to improve lives and positively impact society.　① ② ③ ④ ⑤

The mindset of an authentic advisor to billionaire families

1. I am dedicated to finding the best solutions for the family I serve within the limitations of the playing field. ① ② ③ ④ ⑤

2. I recognize that consistency in my approach is critical, and I strive to understand the family's goals. ① ② ③ ④ ⑤

3. Protecting the family against false advisors and safeguarding their family story is essential. ① ② ③ ④ ⑤

4. The family and I will seek a better fit if our needs outgrow our current advisors' or service providers' skills and services. ① ② ③ ④ ⑤

5. I am committed to managing risk factors and upholding our professional reputation. ① ② ③ ④ ⑤

6. I value open communication and seek aligned solutions. ① ② ③ ④ ⑤

7. The family's wealth is our shared responsibility, and I am committed to continually improving and sharing my knowledge and skills to enhance the family story. ① ② ③ ④ ⑤

8. My role is that of a dedicated contributor, and I am committed to reflecting on my conduct and seeking support when needed. ① ② ③ ④ ⑤

9. I understand the importance of balancing my role with my personal life and am committed to maintaining a healthy equilibrium. ① ② ③ ④ ⑤

10. I need to be compensated relatively because I have a life and can't focus on my core duties if my bills are unpaid. ① ② ③ ④ ⑤

11. I need time to disconnect and do something that I love. ① ② ③ ④ ⑤

12. I prefer not to make mistakes, but I am human. ① ② ③ ④ ⑤

13. The embarrassment is prominent when I don't have all the answers, but I will find them. ① ② ③ ④ ⑤

Be a leader or be led —
the choice is yours.

The mindset of advisory teams

1. We care. ① ② ③ ④ ⑤

2. We have multiple masters, but ultimately, we function best where our voices are heard and respected. ① ② ③ ④ ⑤

3. Protecting the family against false advisors and safeguarding their family story is essential. ① ② ③ ④ ⑤

4. We have much to offer to improve the destiny of others. ① ② ③ ④ ⑤

5. We are probably working and studying while others are out having a good time. ① ② ③ ④ ⑤

6. We respect knowledge and success. ① ② ③ ④ ⑤

7. We don't feel comfortable when family members don't respect our contributions. ① ② ③ ④ ⑤

8. We make complex advice look easy. ① ② ③ ④ ⑤

LDK — LDK

Your vision ...

What is your vision for the world with the great transfer of wealth?

What is your current landscape?

Who is part of your advisory landscape?

Make your vision count by structured philanthropic solutions

Successful families, know how to create something greater than themselves. It is often observed that people who inherit wealth are hesitant to donate to charity. However, they are more interested in supporting sustainable and philanthropic initiatives. While there are several well-known cases of billionaire entrepreneurs pledging most of their fortunes to philanthropic causes, it needs to be discovered that those with inherited wealth seem more reticent. Most first-generation billionaires considered following their philanthropic goals and impacting the world as a primary objective of their legacy, whereas less than a third of the inheriting generations did so.

The impact of unique views on philanthropic solutions

Each generation has its unique way of making a difference. With the rapid advancement of technology, younger generations, such as *Millennials* and *Generation Z*, are less likely to limit their philanthropic efforts to traditional donations. They see social media and online fundraising as effective avenues for positive change. In contrast, Boomers, who grew up during a different time, believed that participating in marches and making charitable donations were some of the only ways to make a meaningful impact.

What is your vision for philanthropy?

In your opinion what will the future of philanthropy look like?

What is the impact that you have made through your giving efforts?

What immediate actions can you take to create a better world?

What conversations will you have to move closer to living a meaningful life for yourself and others?

> *I genuinely enjoy conversing with people and believe it's an art becoming less common. Engaging in meaningful conversations is a simple yet powerful act.*
>
> *In today's world, where many people are isolated, taking the initiative to reach out and connect with others can help build strong relationships and create a sense of community within the family office and multi-generational wealth systems.*
>
> Brian DeLucia

BONUS LIST

Family philanthropy

> *The world is a mountain in which*
> *your words are echoed back to you.*
> Rumi

Philanthropy framework

Philanthropy is a proven way to build deep and meaningful changes and conversations. However, family philanthropy can be challenging as each generation is drawn to different causes and has other ideas about deploying wealth to support those causes.

Legal structures

Families may establish legal structures based on their goals, like a registered charity.

Framework

Families can also create or incorporate the philanthropy framework as a separate document or incorporate it into a *Family Charter* that outlines principles of governance for philanthropy.

Principles

The principles essential for family philanthropy are:

- Transparency and accountability.

- Clearly defined roles and responsibilities.

- Effective communication and decision-making processes.

- Conflict resolution mechanisms.

Effective participation

To effectively participate in charitable and philanthropic causes, it is essential to consider a few things.

- Start by defining your philanthropic objectives and the causes and sectors you wish to support, such as education and the environment, in addition to causes that align with a past experience within your family.

- Consider whether you want to partner with anyone or any existing organizations.

Type and frequency of contributions

Additionally, deciding what type of donations you want to make and how frequently is essential.

Consider the impact

Consider the possibility of impact investing or exploring other ways of giving back. Decide how you would like to be involved and how you will define your ongoing goals and role and that of your family.

Level of engagements

Unpack and understand the level of your engagements for real change and impact and how this will play out in your day-to-day activities and overall strategies. Define what is essential to you from a privacy point of view and whether you would like to retain your privacy. Consider your communication strategy or style.

Causes or organizations that you wish to support

It is also essential to decide which types of causes or charities you do not wish to support, which should be out of scope, and define the restrictions for these.

Decide on your end goal or aim, including when you would like to terminate your support, the organization that you formed, or if there is no need to have an end goal.

Management and oversight

The management and oversight function must be reviewed and monitored to determine how this works. Consider whether there are any conflicts of interest and how these must be dealt with or recorded.

Expert support

Decide how you will align with expert support, to provide guidance and help with the governance / administration / reporting and requirements. The question that arises is: how you will select them? Expert advice must be aligned with family values.

Budget requirements

Finally, decide on your budget requirements and who will keep track of the spending. Determine who has financial oversight and how this should be done or recorded.

MY wish for our family's philanthropy ...

My favorite quote on making a difference is:

Our family values are:

Our family vision:

Our family mission is:

My dream for our family is:

Create dreams for a better world ...

The Other Side of the Rainbow
Selected extracts from a song by Melba Moore

My friend, what's on your mind?
Tell me where you want to go.
Your greatest dreams can take you there.
Don't give up if the dreams deferred.

Remember if you don't follow your dreams,
you'll never know
what's on the other side of the rainbow.
You'll never know
what you will find at the top of the mountain.
You'll never know
where you will be at your journey's end.

Now someone will try to bring you down.
They'll say, "Dreams are for those who sleep."
Oh but dreamers posses great powers untold.
They build worlds others cannot see.

Look within your heart
and your dreams will come true.
Don't let nobody tell ya
(nobody tell you)
what's impossible for you.
Don't let nobody tell ya
(nobody tell you)
what you got to do.

Remember if you don't follow your dreams,
you'll never know
what's on the other side of the rainbow, and you'll never know
what you will find at the top of the mountain.
You'll never know
where you will be at your journey's end.

....

Formulating a definition of family and acknowledging its significance is crucial to establishing your family office. This practice ultimately provides a sense of security for your family. It streamlines the administration of wealth and protective tactics and shapes your philanthropy mission within the family office.

Anne Klein

No two families are the same, yet each has individuals whose perspectives on philanthropy and its relationship to their business and family office operations deserve to be acknowledged, valued, and grasped because they impact the family story.

Anne Klein

Chapter 1

Global Wealth Dynamics –
An Overview

The wealth landscape is poised for ongoing transformation in response to market dynamics and the ever-changing needs of the families they serve. Notably, strategic asset allocation will continue to command significant attention. Pertinent concerns for family offices in the foreseeable future encompass climate change, the debt landscape, and geopolitical conflicts. Additionally, challenges related to inflation and interest rates warrant careful consideration.

Geographical asset allocations are debated, but a strong preference for domestic investments remains in countries like the USA, Switzerland, and other countries in Europe. Family offices are increasingly confident in active management, using this approach and careful manager selection to enhance portfolio diversification. Notably, sustainability has emerged as a pivotal element in risk assessment for family offices. With climate change gaining global recognition as a critical issue, sustainability is seen as a key driver of risks and opportunities for operational businesses and investment portfolios.

Some family offices are increasingly worried about their exposure to natural disasters and the insurance market. They believe that the current property coverage for natural disasters is expensive. As the requirements for sustainability become more complex, partly due to regulatory measures in sectors like real estate, family offices are voicing a more vital need for advanced information and advice. They are particularly keen on their role as investment specialists, placing it above all other priorities.

Many family offices' operational focus is predominantly on internal investment activities rather than encompassing the full spectrum of tasks to support families. Most family offices not only formulate investment decisions but also oversee their execution. Furthermore, their primary emphasis is on financial rather than non-financial risks.

Since most family offices operate with minimal staff, venturing beyond their core responsibilities presents potential challenges. Family offices vary widely across regions, primarily influenced by local macroeconomics, legislative requirements, and the specific goals and preferences of the families involved.

Tech companies have a leading role in the generative AI revolution. On average, family offices have strategically invested in North American asset classes, leveraging the region's resilience to high policy rates and geopolitical risks. Moreover, they foresee AI's productivity gains as a solution to global labor shortages.

Although the family office landscape will continue to grow and evolve, their curiosity will always bring them back to specific themes and new opportunities. Deep tech, health tech, biotechnology, and medical devices spark growing interests. Regional differences, family dynamics, and strategies will always impact how a family office views various endeavors.

1 In the global spotlight

Each region of the family office and generational society will have differences and similarities; their willingness to invest time and expertise into workable solutions will enhance their future sustainability.

The old, the new, and the forgotten landscapes

A prominent issue is the competition among major global financial centers to appeal to new and established family offices, involving locations such as Singapore and Hong Kong.

1.1 United States of America

There are numerous single-family offices in the United States, with a significant concentration in New York City.

As the country's financial hub, New York has a high percentage of family offices, followed by California and Texas at 16% North America dominates the Ultra-High-Net-Worth (UHNW) population.

1.2 Latin America

Family offices in Latin America are mainly located in the region's major cities, such as Mexico City, Sao Paulo, Buenos Aires, and Santiago. However, family offices are also established in smaller cities and towns, particularly in Colombia, Peru, and Chile.

1.3 Europe

Although the term *family office* originated in the United States, the concept of general offices or gatekeepers can be traced back to Europe. Family offices are still crucial in Europe.

1.4 United Kingdom

The United Kingdom is home to Europe's fastest-growing tech hub. Zuckerberg's family office, Iconiq, opened in London. The firm is positioning itself to capture venture capital deals for growth-stage tech start-ups in the region.

1.5 Middle East

The Middle East is home to a significant population of ultra-high-net-worth (UHNW) individuals and families. This wealth has led to the growth of Family offices dedicated to serving UHNW families in the region. Middle Eastern family offices embody unique features that shape their operational dynamics, standing at the intersection of tradition and modernity.

1.6 Asia

The 2023 *Global Family Office Compensation Benchmark Report* estimates that there are approximately 20,000 family offices worldwide, with 9% based in Asia. Singapore remains a favored global family office hub in Asia, while Hong Kong aims to attract 200 large family offices by 2025.

1.7 Africa

A growing number of affluent individuals and billionaires in Africa are considering establishing a dedicated entity to oversee the management of their families' wealth and affairs. While many entrust the responsibility to multi-family offices and private banks, a select few have chosen to establish single-family offices to cater specifically to the needs of their immediate and extended families.

1.8 Offshore jurisdictions

Furthermore, many family offices are set up in offshore jurisdictions, such as the Cayman Islands and the British Virgin Islands.

This trend is driven by a desire to take advantage of favorable tax and regulatory regimes and to diversify geographic risk.

2 Legacy counts for more than what meets the eye

We believe legacy is more than money,
social status, and material things.
It's about the depth of our contribution
to the planet and humanity,
and how we cultivate connections
with the people who matter the most.
Wellth Works.

Every family has goals and objectives, but we can all learn from one another to reach the next level. Most successful families have invested their time and resources to establish and improve their legacy, which is not limited to the value on the balance sheet. There will always be differences in attitudes towards family wealth and generational and cultural disparities.

However, wealth does grant you certain liberties, and at the same time, it places responsibility on the guardians of wealth. These shared values bind families together and guide their legacy planning.

2.1 Generational realities

The approach to wealth management varies across generations. First-generation wealth creators often lean towards conservative investments, while their successors may opt for riskier ventures. These choices are not just about financial strategies; they reflect the evolving dynamics and values within the family.

2.2 Different families do things differently

Families must be mindful of their actions' impact on environmental and social issues. Some families and generations may focus on creating an effect, while others may concentrate on matters closer to their purpose. The new wealth owners are usually more conscious of these issues, and their actions can contribute to a more sustainable and equitable future.

2.3 Establish the story you wish to tell

Values and objectives play a pivotal role in shaping a family's legacy. Each family has a unique story to tell, and by investing time and resources into establishing and building a legacy, they can make a lasting impact that transcends generations and cultural differences. Families can carefully plan and consider their values and objectives to ensure their legacy reflects their future goals and aspirations.

2.4 Don't miss any thematic trends

Generative artificial intelligence is anticipated to be the predominant investment focus for family offices, with health tech, automation, and robotics closely following suit. Regional disparities in industry dominance further influence investment trends.

Rewrite your story to make it count, enhance it for clarity and impact, create a structure, and transform it for the family office world.

3 Enhancing efficiencies

Enhancing efficiencies prevents failure through the lens of the family office landscape, from Africa to the United States of America and beyond.

Do it trembling if you must, but do it!
Emmet Fox

3.1 Back to basics: family governance

Many families start with a basic structure using a trust, mainly a legal governance structure. A family office covers more of the macro or broad range of what is performed through the office, for example, governance, investments, healthcare planning, personal needs, accounting, security, etc. The term **family office** has many elements; the definitions are comprehensive, and how people understand the term varies from the lenses they use to examine and measure it.

Family offices can generally be classified as single-family offices, multi-family offices, embedded family offices, virtual family offices, or diverse options. The definitions of *family offices* are broad and unique and consider a range of

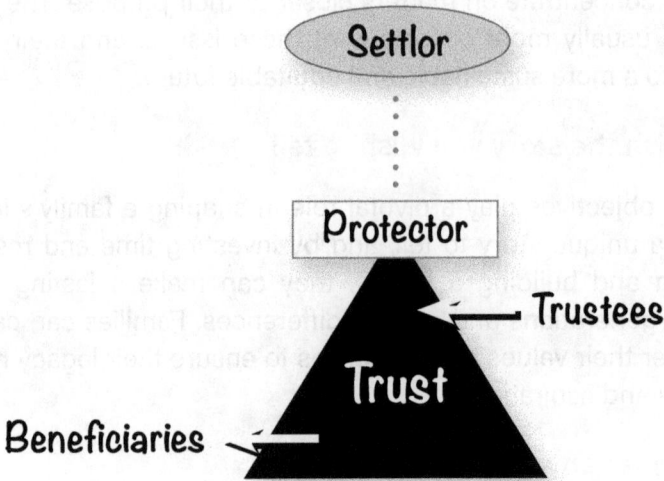

Figure 1: Basic Structure for family governance

factors, such as the industry that the family operates in, the countries they are interested in, their location, and expansion plans.

Flexibility is crucial, and any structure that does not allow for adaptability or fluidity will eventually impact the effectiveness of the family office.

3.2 Basic types of family office terminology

The two main types of family offices are *single-family (SFOs)* and *multi-family (MFOs) offices*, which differ in several aspects, such as structure, client base, and leadership and management approach.

The SFO is a family office designed to serve a single family, whether established by the family directly or by an external entity managing it on behalf of the family.

On the other hand, an MFO operates similarly to a wealth management firm but also offers non-investment services catering to families ranging from 80 to 100+ families. These services can be provided domestically or cross-border.

4 Wealthy people

A person leaves a reputation as a swallow leaves its call.

From the 32nd chapter of Legend of Heroes

Although there is a need for a clear criterion to identify wealth, global and domestic standards still need to be implemented. The standards for identifying high-net-worth individuals (HNWIs) vary internationally, from region to region, for e.g. it ranges from US$30 million to US$50 million, with anything between US$50 -US$100 million considered ultra-high-net worth, in certain places.

Wealthy individuals typically have multiple residences, invest in various businesses, and have diverse interests across the globe.

As of December 2022, the United States of America has the highest number of HNWIs, with 5.3 million individuals. Most HNWIs in the United States reside in California, Texas, New York, Florida, and Illinois. New York City has the largest concentration of HNWIs among all cities globally, with 340,000 individuals.

Although HNWIs account for only 0.003% of the world's population, they possess 13% of its total wealth. As of 2017, 226,450 individuals were classified as Ultra-High-Net-Worth Individuals (UHNWI), and their combined total wealth grew to US$27 trillion.

4.1 The billionaire landscape

It's not who I am underneath but what I do that defines me.

Batman, Batman Begins

In 2022, factors such as the global pandemic, the European conflict, rising inflation, and initiating a new monetary tightening cycle created highly challenging conditions.

The total net worth of the billionaire class experienced a decline of 5.5%, dropping to US$11.1 trillion in 2022. This marked the second-largest annual decrease in the past decade, although it could only partially offset the substantial increase in billionaire wealth in 2021.

Families who adopt an organized and forward-thinking approach are more likely to successfully navigate the challenges and unpredictability that life may present, allowing them to adapt and thrive in different situations.

4.2 World's first trillionaire

Should we shift our focus from the billionaires to the first trillionaires? Will the first trillionaires be Musk or Bezos? *Will they be someone who masters AI and apply it in new ways?*

*What are **your** predictions to the trillionaire universe?*

Could the first trillionaire come from Africa? What are your thoughts?

From which industry will the wealth be created?

4.3 The Africa wealth landscape

According to recent estimates, private wealth in Africa was valued at approximately US$2.0 trillion in December 2020.

The top five wealth markets in Africa are South Africa, Egypt, Nigeria, Morocco, and Kenya, which account for over 50% of the continent's total wealth. In terms of wealth per capita, Mauritius is the wealthiest country in Africa. The World Bank designated it as a high-income country in July 2020.

4.4 The Covid-19 pandemic

The COVID-19 pandemic has indeed impacted private wealth and the levels of high-net-worth individuals (HNWIs) in Africa, leading to a 9% decrease in 2020. However, the future holds promise.

Total private wealth in Africa is projected to increase by a significant 30% and reach US$ 2.6 trillion by 2030. This growth will be driven by solid expansion in the billionaire and centi-millionaire segments, particularly in rapidly growing economies such as Ethiopia, Mauritius, Rwanda, Kenya, and Uganda.

4.5 The financial landscape that defines our world

At the top of the wealth pyramid, a small group of 59 million people owns 46% of the world's total wealth, which equals an astonishing US$208 trillion. These 59 million people represent only 1.3% of the world's population. The global upper-middle class comprises 51,549,760 individuals, each with a net worth ranging from US$1 million to US$5 million.

Financial security and opportunities vary significantly worldwide. Economic situations are remarkably diverse, with 642 million individuals having a net worth between US$100,000 and $1 million and 1.8 billion individuals having a net worth between US$10,000 and US$100,000.

Unfortunately, economic challenges persist for the largest group, which includes 2.8 billion individuals at the base tier with a net worth below US$10,000. From a broader perspective, 5.4 billion individuals contribute to the global wealth landscape, creating a collective force of US$454 trillion.

This vivid picture of the financial landscape that defines our world should inspire a sense of global economic awareness.

5 Finding the pathway to family office success

Don't be afraid to fail. It's not the end of the world;
in many ways, it's the first step toward learning something
better and getting better at it.

Jon Hamm

5.1 Total balance sheet management, consolidated reporting

It is crucial to have a comprehensive list of critical topics related to family wealth management.

These topics include identifying potential risks and challenges, developing asset protection and tax planning strategies, and ensuring successful management and preservation of family wealth and assets for future generations.

Families and their advisory teams must thoroughly understand their unique financial situation and goals through open and collaborative discussions.

This approach allows for personalized and practical solutions tailored to specific needs.

Topics worth considering in any family wealth management plan:

◆   Succession planning.

◆   Diversification of non-domestic assets.

◆   Access to unique investment opportunities.

◆   Family office arrangements, trusted advice, key relationships, and gatekeepers

◆   Emigration and global challenges.

◆   Mediation and family charters, guidance to successive generations (inter-generational estate planning).

◆   Death of the patriarch or matriarch.

◆   Consolidation of assets, business strategies, and reporting.

◆   Philanthropy.

◆   Guidance on marital regimes for successive generations.

◆   Global footprint.

◆   Family values.

These factors must be considered when managing wealth and planning for a family's future. Combining advisory expertise creates a comprehensive plan that covers these topics and other concerns.

To find a successful pathway, it is important to recognize and use the valuable knowledge and wisdom, as it is gained. Its purpose is to inspire discussions and promote thoughtful decision-making.

5.2 Collaboration changes dynamics

Specialists collaborating within their professional spheres improve the world by promoting curiosity and expanding knowledge-sharing. They advance the sector to thrive and integrate different perspectives and dynamics within the family office stakeholder network. This creates a stronger bond between the families and the professional advisors through their experience in various global and exclusive conversations.

The conversations should be similar to cricket, not golf, even if the industry loves playing golf. Hear the other side.

Anne Klein

Family offices and their advisers often need more alignment and the first step toward achieving this is through open discussions and the willingness to freely share knowledge and wisdom.

LDK ⦿ LDK

Some switches to ponder ...

Generation one to generation "eternity"	Sick to healthy
Client to advisor	Healthy to sick
Unaware to aware	Good relationships to toxic relationships
Unconscious to conscious	Passive to active
Owner to observer	Young to old
No family structure to the first level of structure	Driven by fear to powered by love
Structure to multi-family office	Lack to abundance
Multi-family office to single-family office	Abuse to peace
Life to death	War to peace
Passive to active family members	Internal talk to external discussions
Risk to minimizing risk	Risk to risk profiling
Conversation to action	Tolerance to intolerance
Unsustainable to sustainable	No dream to unlimited dreams
Knowledge to application	Family to the community to humanity
Knowledge to practicality	No legacy to a divine legacy
Married to divorced	Family to a dynasty
Unmarried to married	Healthy mind to an unhealthy mind
Childless to children to grandchildren	Good habits to poor habits
No children to step-children	No married-ins to married-ins
Rich to poor	Physics to quantum physics
Poor to rich	Real assets to digital assets
One type of asset to a different kind of asset	Real conversations to imaginary conversations
Business family to wealthy family or both	No money to a millionaire
Charity to philanthropic	Solvency to insolvency
Philanthropic to impact	Millionaire to billionaire
One jurisdiction to another	Hero to zero
One advisor to another	Zero to hero
No structure to structure	Parent to child to parent-child
One average conversation to multiple-quality conversations	Able to disable
No governance to governance	No security to security
Cash to cashless	No control to calculated control
No context to context	No power to power to personal power
Knowledge to applied knowledge	Taker to giver to participant
CEO to Chairperson	Voiceless to a seat at the table
Rich to ultra-rich	No table to own table
Family to cast out	No participation to participation
Word to action	**What's your Switch?**

Chapter 2

Family Offices
An insightful perspective

The *family office community* is at a point of significant transformation, and even experienced family offices need to reset their best practices on the governance side and adjust their strategies. The interconnectedness of the family office landscape has revolutionized family wealth conversations.

A good plan violently executed now
is better than a perfect plan executed next week.
George S Patton

Examining the family structure, struggles, priorities, and issues from another angle can lead to different outcomes for becoming and staying prosperous.

We each have a voice and
are proxy holders for a better tomorrow.
Anne Klein

How one acquires wealth and how wealth is dealt with, shared, and experienced is often a personal story. Acquiring wealth can lead to different outcomes depending on the support and advice received and actions or inactions that flow from that. Successful families have demonstrated that taking the initiative to establish the family's values, mission, and vision can guide future generations toward a fulfilling life.

1 History of family offices

John D. Rockefeller is widely credited with establishing the United States' first full-service, single family office. The **Rockefeller Family Office** was established in 1882 and provided diverse services, including investment management, estate planning, and philanthropy.

The **Rockefeller Family Office** was a model for other wealthy families, and soon, more family offices emerged, such as the Carnegie and Vanderbilt families.

Lost fortunes ...

> *"Any fool can make a fortune;*
> *it takes a man of brains to hold onto it"*
> Commodore Vanderbilt is said to have told his son
> William Henry "Billy" Vanderbilt (Young Billy).

Cornelius Vanderbilt, also known as "Commodore" Vanderbilt, launched his family's business in 1810 by borrowing US$100 from his mother. Initially, he operated a passenger boat on Staten Island and later expanded into steamboats.

He then established his railroad empire in New York Central, whose tracks covered the United States and gave him a monopoly for all rail services in and out of New York City. By the time he died in 1877, Vanderbilt had reportedly amassed a $100 million fortune, more than what was held in the U.S. Treasury.

Young Billy inherited the family's 87% stake in New York Central and doubled the fortune to over US$200 million. Billy died in 1885; he left the family's stake in the company to his sons, Cornelius Vanderbilt II and William Kissam Vanderbilt.

The division of the Vanderbilt fortune in the third generation coincided with a decline in family interest in New York Central — and a gradual increase in spending.

During the Gilded Age, there was much spending and endless rallies to maintain appearances. The Vanderbilt family had many valuable assets, including an impressive art collection of old masters, several Newport, Rhode Island houses like The Breakers, and ten mansions on Fifth Avenue in Manhattan.

While the Vanderbilt family may not have made Forbes' inaugural America's Richest Families list, their influence endures through Vanderbilt University in Nashville, Tennessee, and Vanderbilt Avenue in New York's Manhattan and Brooklyn, serving as tangible reminders of their historical significance.

2 Role of family influences

The Astor family rose to prominence in the business, society, and politics of the United States and the United Kingdom during the 19th and 20th centuries. Though their roots are German, some of their ancestors originated from the Italian and Swiss Alps.

The Astors settled in Germany and arrived in North America in the 18th century with John Jacob Astor, considered one of the wealthiest individuals in history. Astor called his wife, "the best business partner any man ever had." Astor's wife was so good at the business that she charged her husband US$500 an hour.

3 Evolution of family wealth

In the 1900s, family offices became more prevalent, and wealthy families established offices to manage their wealth. By the 1970s, private banking, customized services, and multi-family offices had evolved, providing a range of services to meet the needs of wealthy families.

These offices became more sophisticated over time, and by the 1990s, family offices started offering a broader range of services, such as tax planning, risk management, and family governance.

4 Family offices in South Africa

Family offices have been introduced previously, but South Africa needs a more formal recorded history. Prominent families with strong enterprise leads are believed to have established embedded family offices. These offices were later separated as independent operations, and most families have international links and advisors. The decision to split the family office from the enterprise entities was made to ensure independence and avoid conflict of interest.

In doing so, the families could manage their wealth more securely and efficiently, with separate teams dedicated to each function.

4.1 Most powerful and richest families in South Africa in 2024

The South African economy is widely recognized as one of the most dynamic economies in Africa, with many companies operating across a broad range of industries. As expected in such a thriving economy, several individuals and families have accumulated vast fortunes and gained considerable influence. So, which families are the most affluent and influential in South Africa today?

The wealthiest and most powerful families in South Africa have diversified their investments in different sectors across the country and globally, often operating conglomerates. Some families have invested in the lucrative mining industry, while others own stakes in financial institutions.

4.2 A story of resilience

A story of resilience for one South African family enterprise, taking a different path to success.

From the Spanish flu to Covid-19

In 1918, the world was grappling with the Spanish flu pandemic and the aftermath of World War 1. Eskort, a company, had its challenges during this time. Its inaugural annual general meeting had to be postponed due to the influenza sweeping the globe. This was a testament to the global turmoil of the era.

Fast-forward to a century later, in 2024, and Eskort stands as a beacon of light. It has navigated more than a century of change, challenges, and growth, surviving two pandemics and thriving, thanks to the unwavering commitment of its people, the family values that underpin the company, and the dedicated leadership.

4.3 Family offices further away from home

Please don't spend time beating on a wall,
hoping to transform it into a door.

Coco Chanel

Location, location

Many wealthy families establish their own family offices in various locations worldwide. While some regions are more familiar with family offices, such as the United States and Canada, family-driven enterprises exist globally, from the United Kingdom and Europe to Africa and Asia. However, due to the rising cost of operations in certain places like Singapore, wealthy families are considering options such as setting up single family offices or different alternatives. This may result in the merging or adoption of alternative models for single family offices in places like Singapore.

Hong Kong

Hong Kong has more than 2,700 single family offices, making it a thriving hub for family wealth management. The city has a long history of managing family wealth dating back to the late 1800s, making it a significant part of the asset management sector.

Over the years, Hong Kong has become one of Asia's largest cross-border wealth management centers. The city has recently invested more resources into developing a world-class family office regime with an enhanced investment strategy. Many high-net-worth individuals have chosen to set up their family offices in Hong Kong, as they value their privacy and prefer to maintain a low profile.

Global wealth

Today, family offices are a vital part of the global wealth industry, and they continue to evolve to meet the changing needs of wealthy families. They provide a range of services, from investment management and philanthropy to estate planning and family governance, and they are an essential tool for managing and preserving wealth across generations.

Deep-rooted history

The idea of family offices originated in the West. However, "majordomos" were appointed in ancient China to manage family matters. family offices in Europe are rooted in royal and noble households. Prominent families appointed stewards in the Middle Ages to oversee their lands, finances, and legal matters. These stewards acted on behalf of the family, ensuring the preservation and transfer of wealth to future generations.

5 An insider's take, trends, and opportunities: Options based on needs and growth

It takes as much energy to wish as it does to plan.
Eleanor Roosevelt

Families have a range of options for establishing a family office. Identifying the right people and service providers is essential to ensure success. Families are advised to verify and periodically review their service providers as these determine the scope of family office activities and services.

Families and advisors must understand the family's unique needs and identify the services required, from concierge to general services. Mapping out the needs, responsibilities, and critical focus areas is crucial to maintaining the family office's effectiveness.

5.1 Family offices have tripled since 2019, leading to a new gold rush on Wall street

On the rise

Various reports reveal that the number of family offices worldwide are on the rise, with a significant concentration in North America.

Family offices worldwide have tripled since 2019, creating a new wave of competition among private equity firms, hedge funds, and venture capital firms to attract investments.

Experts suggest that family offices now manage trillions of USD, and their numbers are continuously growing. This shows that the investment world is constantly evolving, and businesses must keep up with the pace to stay ahead of the curve.

Billionaires, but what about the trillionaires?

With over 2,600 billionaires worldwide, nearly all requiring a family office. The typical threshold for a family office, the number of people in the world worth $100 million or more, has surged to over 90,000. This means there is still plenty of potential for growth in this industry. The family office boom has attracted private equity firms and other alternative managers seeking to raise funds.

We must wait and see how the family office will function in the *Trillion Dollar Family Office* space.

Define what the term family office means to you.

A single family office is a holistic,
full-balance-sheet wealth management solution
for an affluent individual or family.
Richard. C Wilson

5.2 Single family offices (SFOs)

Family offices are advisory firms that focus on managing the wealth and private affairs of ultra-high-net-worth individuals (UHNWI). Unlike traditional wealth management firms, they provide a comprehensive outsourced solution for managing affluent individuals' or families' financial and investment aspects.

A family office is an abstract concept in unusual ways. The term *Family Office* should be used with caution. It can be an unclear concept and 'mysterious' at times. The onus is on the reader to apply the insights provided to suit their unique circumstances. It is imperative to recognize that family offices can be complex entities that vary significantly in structure, services, and composition.

By adopting a nuanced approach to the subject matter and seeking to understand the complexities inherent in family offices, we can develop a more comprehensive understanding of how these entities operate and how they can be optimized to serve the needs of families effectively.

5.3 Understand what the term *family office* might mean to others

Bermuda's Minister of Economy and Labour, Jason Hayward, introduced the framework for the solutions for family offices in the House of Assembly. In its simplest form, the Minister said that a family office is a private business established to benefit a family of significant wealth.

With a heavy focus on private wealth management, family offices manage critical areas of family assets such as securities and investment funds, real estate holdings, tax matters, and estate management. Family offices also serve as the central hub for a family's legacy, governance, and succession and often support the education and development of family members, coordinate communications, and resolve issues within the family enterprise.

5.4 Wider than the family

Family offices also facilitate charitable and philanthropic activities that help sustain a family's legacy. Many influential figures use family offices to manage wealth while driving philanthropy. Michael Jordan, Oprah Winfrey, and Bill Gates are examples of influential people whose family offices helped shape their enduring legacies and catalyzed societal and economic changes.

5.5 Frameworks set by governments

Some countries have specific legislation regrading family offices, and most recently, according to Minister Hayward, "Bermuda boasts an attractive framework for family offices that stands out from other jurisdictions. Our strong asset protection, tax efficiency, political stability, and well-defined regulatory regimes are some ways Bermuda has set itself apart from its competitors. Our framework includes a unique mixture of a best-in-class financial services regulatory regime that facilitates access to Investment opportunities in innovative digital assets, emerging technologies, and innovative insurance solutions. Government support further enhances the family office framework."

Curiosity and the family office world

Gaining a higher perspective is crucial for empowering families and advisors to make informed decisions before delving into intricate details and minor aspects.

Fame and wealth without wisdom are unsafe possessions.
Democritus

Curiosity, from private markets to public interest, is a crucial element that drives success and sustainable wealth development for family offices. Family wealth dynamics depend on factors such as the evolution of generational wealth. For example, a third-generation representative of an entrepreneurial family may have different drivers than a 16th-generational participant.

Sensitivity and confidentiality are non-negotiable elements that create harmony when dealing with the family office ecosystem. Even when families and advisors must make bold decisions, including performing a strategic gap analysis, everything must remain centered on the family's well-being, values, and mission statement.

6 Types of family offices

6.1 Single family offices

Affluent families often seek professional support and services to manage and preserve their wealth while retaining their identity. This necessitates strategies and solutions, such as comprehending and documenting family wealth, history, and objectives, tracking and managing wealth within the family wealth ecosystem, and creating a single family office.

Investment of time and resources

Establishing a single family office solution requires a significant investment of time and resources. Due to the dedicated resources and significant family office costs, industry experts typically recommend a minimum of US$100 million in investable assets to develop a single family office.

Families can benefit from favorable economies of scale by reaching this asset threshold.

Complexity Oversight

Single family offices are designed to oversee greater complexity and provide aligned services to the family's needs. These offices offer elevated levels of privacy and confidentiality, with controlled access to information and coordinated work with advisors. However, setting up and maintaining a single family office can be expensive, involving hiring skilled professionals, investing in technology, and managing operational costs. These costs are often charged back to the family clients. Governance, compliance, and reporting concerns must also be addressed.

Analysis

The decision to establish a family office must be based on a thorough analysis of the benefits and costs of doing so. While family offices can provide significant advantages for managing wealth and supporting a family's needs, they also require a substantial investment of resources. Setting up a family office requires careful consideration and evaluation of the options, as well as seeking guidance from experts in the field.

Establishing a single family office

When establishing a family office, critical considerations require a comprehensive tax, legal, and practical framework aligned with the family's needs. Finding a structure that ensures the family office's longevity, provides expansion opportunities, and protects the family from potential financial or other risks is essential. Additionally, aligning services and advisors, creating tailored solutions, and catering to the family's lifestyle needs are crucial.

The regulatory approvals include licenses, permits, and other legal documentation necessary to comply with the jurisdiction's laws.

Operating model

When establishing a family office, it is crucial to have a comprehensive understanding of the operating model that best suits the family's needs. To achieve this, it is prudent to have access to a team of professionals who can provide expert guidance in choosing a suitable model.

The team should consist of talented individuals who can provide sound advice and clear guidelines to support the family with communication methods, preferences, and short-, long- and medium-term strategies.

Policies and procedures

The in-house policies and procedures cover a wide range of aspects, from outsourcing specific services to defining governing principles that dictate the use of certain assets, determining family values, and establishing who qualifies as a family member.

Building clear policies and procedures is a essential to the family's governance. This will involve documenting the treasury policies and procedures to ensure the family office operates smoothly. Performing employee background checks and due diligence reviews on other providers regarding family wealth. This can be outsourced to professional companies, providing more comprehensive and reliable results.

Triggers to establish a single family office ...

Liquidity event

A significant liquidity event, such as the sale of a business or a recapitalization, can lead families to consider setting up a family office. Such events can result in a sudden influx of wealth and complex financial matters that require careful management.

A family office can help families navigate these complexities and ensure that the family's wealth is managed effectively for future generations.

The need for separation

Families may consider establishing a family office when other ways of managing their wealth and family ecosystem are no longer effective. This can happen when one uses an "invisible" embedded model for family enterprise personnel to perform family office tasks, causing friction and necessitating a departure to mitigate conflicts of interest and other specific factors unique to the industry and the family.

A family office can help families develop new and more effective strategies for managing their wealth and family matters.

Having substantial levels of wealth

It is recommendable to have family governance structures in place. This will make the transition easier when the family reaches the required amount of investable assets, before establishing a single family office, which can vary depending on their specific needs. However, it is recommended to consider setting up a single family office when the investable assets reach a minimum value of US$100 million. Some experts argue that this threshold should be raised to US$250 million.

6.2 Multi-family offices

Choosing multi-family offices may be optimal for assets between US$20 million and US$100 million. They enable families to access the advantages of a dedicated *single family office* without the total overhead costs and responsibilities. Some providers provide outsourced partners for multi-family offices.

6.3 Embedded family offices

Embedded family offices are a popular starting point for many family businesses because of their efficiency and customizability. An embedded family office is part of the operational side of the family enterprise, which may present challenges if not managed as a separate solution.

However, it can also bring the family enterprise and office closer together. Most families and their advisors will understand when to establish a formal structure for specific trigger events or during a transition.

Family Growth

As family businesses expand and the number of family members involved grows, the complexities of managing wealth, taxes, and other financial responsibilities escalate. Family offices have emerged as a viable option for providing focused coordination and comprehensive support for a family's varying needs.

Family offices can take several forms, including embedded offices integrated within the operating company, single family offices set up outside the company, and third-party multi-family offices serving multiple unrelated families.

6.4 Virtual family offices

Virtual family offices have become increasingly popular and driven by technology. This solution offers a modern approach to servicing families, bringing family office services to a broader audience. To make an informed decision, it is essential to comprehend the cost-effectiveness, service model, delivery methods, vision, value proposition, and pricing.

6.5 Hybrid family offices

Hybrid family offices are created when some family offices combine the characteristics of single and multi-family offices.

7 Characteristics of family offices

7.1 Variety of sizes and services

Family offices can range from small offices, focusing on a single need, to full-service offices providing a wide range of administrative, tax, legal, accounting, and investment services. By leveraging the existing infrastructure of the family enterprise, embedded offices offer cost efficiencies and minimize staff requirements.

Concerns may arise regarding the blurred lines of decision-making, as employees are tasked with the work of the business and the family office. Additionally, privacy concerns may arise as more employees access sensitive family information thereby creating a trigger event to establish a single family office.

7.2 Resilience, global expansion

Family offices are known for their resilience and prefer to align and explore other avenues for sustainability. Advisors from around the world find ways to connect to assist wealthy families. Each country has unique challenges and cultures that must be considered when establishing a family office; local expertise is critical. When affluent families expand globally, connecting local experts with global networks is crucial due to their family and business dynamics.

7.3 Extensive networks

Advisors can access an extensive network of global single and multi-family office communities in certain countries. However, other countries are at varying stages of development. As wealth grows and spreads worldwide, specialized expertise will be essential to support expansion. Family offices prioritize collaboration and exploring alternative options for sustainability.

7.4 New Age founders

*Energy and imagination are
the springboards to wealth creation.*

Brian Tracy

Younger founders have a different risk tolerance, and their investment strategies are often geared towards maximizing wealth growth rather than preserving it.

These family offices tend to invest more in technological innovation and emerging industries.

7.5 Non-financial aspect

> *Money is the most envied but the least enjoyed.*
> *Health is the most enjoyed but the least envied.*
>
> Charles Caleb Colton

7.6 Changing the narrative, why not?

It is becoming increasingly apparent that family offices play a significant non-financial role. Family offices support the notion that each generation plays a key role. However, each generation must be woven into the family tapestry. There are cultural differences globally, and each jurisdiction, family, and business are unique yet simultaneously have multiple points of unity.

Cash-rich

Family offices are characterized as cash-rich and deploy liquidity into various private markets, such as private credit, venture capital, real estate, and private equity.

7.7 Specialized skills

Family offices require highly specialized skills, which are typically outsourced. It is critical to select the proper advisory teams and conduct thorough due diligence to ensure the professional teams have the regulatory and licensing requirements.

Establishing a network of specialists and resources is vital to securing a dedicated team environment.

7.8 Individualized entities

Family offices are highly individualized entities catering to each family's unique needs. Despite the differences, most family offices aim to achieve common objectives, such as creating and maintaining a formal structure for managing family wealth and legacy.

7.9 The host of the family legacy

In addition, family offices are responsible for recording and hosting the family legacy, values, and visions.

They provide access to bespoke services that cater to the family's specific needs, including support for lifestyle management.

8 Use of a Private Trust Company (PTC) for wealth structuring

Families can use privately owned trusts of family trust companies to get trustee services for their family. The PTC doesn't engage in public business; instead, it offers trust and fiduciary services to a specific family, their relatives, and their philanthropic organizations.

The PTC acts as a gatekeeper for wealth, ensuring business continuity and providing access to crucial family decision-makers.

A cohesive interaction with specialists and critical family advisors helps consolidate an approach to complex family structures and business partners. Quick turnaround times, easy access to high-quality services, and complex advice are available.

This is a vehicle for protection against unsolicited approaches.

8.1 Tangible and intangible benefits

The tangible advantages of a PTC are long-term estate planning strategies, with increased privacy, flexibility, control, and asset protection. The board of directors has continuity, and there's increased investment discretion.

Confident philanthropic payments and credit protection are available while avoiding future trustee changes. The intangible benefits of a PTC are the education of the next generations of the family, the promotion of succession planning, family cohesion, and intergenerational cultural succession.

8.2 The role of a protector

Families have different ways to maintain influence and maintain balance regarding the family story. One approach is to use a trust structure. In specific locations, a protector is usually chosen to supervise the trustee's decisions and assess whether they are in the best interests of the beneficiaries. It is suggested that the primary responsibility of a protector is to guarantee that the legal and moral aspects of the trust are upheld.

8.3 Personal finances and risk management, consolidated views

Family offices manage family and personal finances and develop risk management strategies. They aim to have a consolidated view of the family wealth and its management, which includes understanding cash flow planning and potential risks, including currency risks, from a close perspective.

8.4 Economic value, privacy, and confidentiality

Family offices recognize the economic value of finding collective solutions for the family and work towards this goal. Family offices place high importance on guarding the management and maintaining the family's confidentiality and privacy regarding family matters.

8.5 Independent support

Matters can become overwhelming, and seeking independent guidance from a trusted partner within the stakeholder network may be necessary. Finding a partner who understands a family office's dynamics and inner workings can be challenging, but still, having someone who can provide support and engagement is needed.

8.6 Trusted partners, the gatekeeper

Trusted advisors play a vital role in providing answers and insights but also require strategic support to comprehend certain situations entirely.

9 Customization of a family office

Other people's wisdom prevents the king from being called a fool.
African Proverb

Family offices' engagement terms are prepared based on agreed principles, and each family has unique considerations. Key ingredients to niche expertise, records, and supporting specific industries are essential.

10 Composition of family offices

Not what you do for your children but what you have taught them to do for themselves will make them successful human beings.
Ann Landers

Families create family offices for various reasons. One benefit of a structured approach is that parents can show their children the multiple doors available. In the process children become empowered to make informed choices which act as a measure of protection against unwanted influences from 'shark attacks'.

10.1 Peer-to-peer support

Family offices provide a platform for peer-to-peer support and networking, facilitating sharing experiences and identifying prospective mentors and mentees. The role of the family office is dynamic and requires an insider's perspective.

10.2 Multi-skilled, multi-layered support

One moment, the family office may be participating in a signing ceremony to celebrate a significant deal while organizing a family meeting, addressing travel preferences, and resolving personality conflicts.

Continue to fly in the direction of your goals.

*Parents can only give good advice or
guide children on the right path,
but the final shaping of a person's character
lies in their own hands.*

Anne Frank

Openness and embracing an elevated vision are essential to ensure the family office's success. Acknowledging the potential for rapid shifts is critical to thriving in this environment and focusing on key areas while finding best practices.

LDK — LDK

Chapter 3

The Creation of a Family Office

Creating a single family office (SFO) tailored to a family's unique needs and circumstances necessitates careful contemplation and preparation.

To initiate the planning process, prospective families are recommended to appoint a team of motivated family leaders and trusted advisors and engage external specialists as needed.

The following checklist, while not exhaustive, serves as a valuable guideline to initiate the planning process:

♦ Conduct a comprehensive family assessment to ascertain the family's financial goals, values, and objectives.

♦ Establish a well-defined governance structure that outlines the roles and responsibilities of family members, trustees, and advisors.

♦ Develop an investment policy statement that reflects the family's investment objectives, risk tolerance, and asset allocation strategies.

♦ Determine the family's reporting and communication requirements, including the frequency and content of reports.

♦ Establish a risk management and compliance framework that safeguards the family's assets, protects against fraud, and ensures regulatory compliance.

It is important to note that the checklist above provides a helpful starting point for families looking to establish a single family office (SFO), but it is a partial list, that will be influenced by the family story, the industry they operate in, as well as the country in which they are based.

1 Time to reflect ...

Families considering setting up an SFO should take ample time to reflect on its purpose and role within the family structure. One of the most critical early tasks in establishing an SFO is to define the family office's mission.

A concise and focused mission statement can guide the SFO's operations and prevent *mission intervention* in the future. To create a mission statement that is both practical and useful, families can seek the help of professional consultants. This statement will help guide the work of the SFO for generations to come and ensure it is aligned with the family's goals and values.

2 The impact of operation businesses and asset allocation

The presence of a connected operating business impacts family offices' investment decisions. Family offices with a related operating business tend to have a lower risk appetite and invest less in public and private equity than those without such a business.

However, family offices with operating companies in the start-up/growth stages tend to invest more in direct private equity while maintaining lower fixed income and cash allocations.

2.1 Identifying the requirements and objectives

Identifying the requirements and objectives that the single family office (SFO) will cater to is imperative. This will ensure that the SFO's structure aligns with the family's goals and objectives. In the planning and development phase of establishing a family office, three critical discussion points must be addressed:

2.2 Who are the "clients" that the SFO will serve?

It is crucial to define the individuals and entities the SFO will serve. A comprehensive project list should include all individuals and entities, such as family branches, investment entities, businesses, trusts, trust companies, and foundations that require support and will be able to access the SFO team.

The design of the SFO should consider each client's unique needs and requirements as well as their influence over it.

2.3 What assets will the SFO manage?

Once the clients have been identified, the SFO needs to unpack all the assets and the liabilities it will manage, oversee and report on. These may include marketable securities, hedge funds, Master Limited Partnerships, direct investments, oil and gas leases, operating businesses, residential and commercial real estate, farms/ranches, collections, aircraft, yachts, horses, and sports teams. The SFO must hire or outsource the expertise needed to oversee and manage the assets.

2.4 What support is required by the "clients"?

The SFO must identify the necessary services that the family office "clients" will need. These services may include investment management, tax, estate planning, philanthropic, and lifestyle management services. The SFO must ensure it has the necessary resources and expertise to provide support and partner with them.

2.5 Investment management services

Families with substantial investments or liquid capital must obtain investment management services. These services may comprise an investment policy statement and asset allocation plan, manager due diligence, and investment reporting.

All SFO clients must acquire comprehensive and accurate performance reporting, accounting, and tax return preparation for each entity, and each of the family members who require these support services.

2.6 Risk management

Coordination of risk management is also essential, including insurance, security, and reputation management. Developing and coordinating estate and tax planning, which may encompass managing a private family trust company, is another crucial necessity for multi-generational families.

Similarly, first-generation entrepreneurs who aim to preserve their families' long-term legacy may require these services and other services that align with their portfolio. Additional services may include property management, staffing, bill payment, and concierge services depending on family needs.

2.7 Where is the shirt?

The adage, "shirt sleeves in three generations," is a well-known fact documented across numerous countries and cultures. Therefore, many wealthy families understand the significance of proper family governance and family wealth-planning strategies during the wealth creator's lifetime. Even after implementing a family governance system, families must continually refine and re-evaluate their values, vision, and mission as their SFO adapts to the family's changing needs and the global environment.

2.8 Business plans

Identifying clients, assets, and needs can lead to developing a business plan. This plan should detail the services to be provided, a short- and long-term timeline, required employees and outsourced talent, service partners needed (for example, custodians, tax counsel, security services), and technology needs.

2.9 Budget requirements

One of the primary objectives in constructing a business plan is determining the budget required for operating a single family office (SFO). It is essential to note that SFOs entail significant costs. However, compared to managing the family's assets through an outsourced or third-party solution, the expense of an SFO may be lower. Furthermore, the return on investment would potentially be much higher due to the SFO's customized approach, which caters to the family's specific needs.

Typically, SFO budgets are calculated as a percentage of the assets under management. The operating costs of an SFO can vary widely, with smaller SFOs managing complex assets costing more than larger SFOs managing a simpler portfolio. This is due to the fewer economies of scale available to exploit.

The budget of an SFO managing an extensive portfolio of alternative investments and commodities for three generations of family members, all of whom, by way of example, share a passion for modern art and house their collections in multiple properties worldwide, would necessarily be more significant in absolute terms and as a percentage of assets under management than the budget of an SFO managing a portfolio of publicly traded securities for a single-family unit. The budget serves as a benchmark for determining expectations for SFO performance.

2.10 The allocation of expenses

When establishing a single family office (SFO) that serves a family spanning multiple generations, it is paramount to consider how the family office should be allocating and charging expenses to clients.

Potential conflicts between family office clients or the family and the office can be forestalled by explicitly outlining the expense allocation method, expected client contributions, and fee collection from the outset by a clearly defined service level agreement.

2.11 Plans

The SFO plan must identify the expertise required to address the client's needs, considering the available budget and the particular assets to be managed. This plan should also indicate whether this expertise will be provided internally or outsourced. With staffing needs established, matters such as location, office space requirements, technology, security, administrative support, and others should be addressed.

2.12 Talent match

Finding the right talent is typically the most daunting aspect of creating an SFO. It is advisable to identify the Chief Executive Officer (CEO) candidate first, if it still needs to be done. The SFO CEO must work closely with the family, the office staff, and external service providers, necessitating excellent organizational, management, and interpersonal skills.

Selecting a CEO based solely on their technical expertise in investing, accounting, or tax planning should be revised. Family members sometimes appoint a trusted advisor or the controller of their operating business who has been loyal to this critical position for many years. However, this can also be a mistake if the trusted advisor or controller cannot scale into the CEO role.

With the CEO performing a high-level executive function and serving as the family's face to the outside world, they will execute the build-out of the SFO by the plan, making the CEO role critical. As a result, candidates should have proven experience successfully leading, managing, and communicating in various complex situations.

2.13 Investment teams

Family offices frequently employ investment team members with substantial prior experience at private banks, investment houses, and hedge funds.

These candidates typically possess highly sought-after skills and may request investment rights or bonus compensation based on investment performance as a condition of employment.

Given the regulations, family offices must exercise caution when structuring such arrangements.

Therefore, SFOs should seek the guidance of seasoned legal counsel when recruiting new investment team members or implementing new strategies.

2.14 Background reviews

All employees, irrespective of their level, should undergo a thorough background check and sign non-compete, non-solicitation, and non-disclosure agreements or whatever agreement the family feels most comfortable with after conversation with their family lawyer. Regardless of the size of the SFO, it should have an employee policy manual. An experienced legal advisor should review and update the manual at least once a year, or from time to time when change is needed.

2.15 Board of Directors

The SFO should be overseen by a board of directors that meets regularly and is responsible for establishing a strategy and managing the CEO. Most families control the board of their SFOs to ensure that the plan aligns with the family's objectives and goals. This choice will entirely depend on the family's vision and the skills required to get the family to the next level. Many SFOs adopt the lead of private enterprises and engage external advisors to join the board and contribute independent viewpoints and expertise.

2.16 Contingency plans

The SFO should prepare a contingency plan that outlines procedures to follow in the event of a natural disaster, extreme market volatility, theft, or technological breach or failure of any kind be it within the family structure or outside of its control.

At a minimum, the contingency plan should provide for the security and safety of the family, its vital information, and tangible assets. It should also safeguard the SFO staff, facilitate off-site data backup, and include a strategy for quickly re-establishing essential office operations off-site. The contingency plan must be drafted and recorded as well as be reviewed as part of the annual compliance reviews.

3 Shifting complex landscapes

If you're going through hell, keep going.

Winston Churchill

3.1 Scenario planning

The landscape of family offices is complex, shaped by various positive and negative triggers that can have significant implications. Each scenario presents an opportunity to make choices, but making informed decisions requires a deep understanding of the situation.

Scenario planning can be a valuable tool for empowering decision-making and ensuring that choices are made quickly and efficiently.

3.2 Navigating complexities

I wear a mask. And that mask,

it's not to hide who I am but to create what I am.

Batman, Comics

Families may consider utilizing a family office solution when the complexity of their overall lives has reached a level where help is needed to "institutionalize" or professionalize their family solutions.

A family office helps families navigate complex legal, financial, and other private and personal matters. It also supports businesses, ensuring their wealth is managed effectively, and their long-term goals are achieved.

Specific patterns can lead to problems. For instance, one person who takes on the role of a self-elected *matriarch* or *patriarch* could cause division among the family or unite them; depending on the agenda, understanding the personal agendas will be a guiding force for the family. As a result, having a plan and an alternative strategy is crucial.

It is also essential to consider the impact of an outsider who has a mandate to act on behalf of the family story.

3.3 Selectively connected

Conversations with external partners can bring fresh perspectives and innovative solutions. This can be particularly useful when trying to limit the impact of a negative situation or when seeking to expand the range of scenarios and outcomes for the family.

Ultimately, having a solid support system and a deep understanding of the family office landscape is critical to making sound decisions and achieving success for future generations.

4 Family office and the legal world

Certain jurisdictions apply specific laws to family offices, which may vary depending on the office's location.

4.1 Jurisdictions and their requirements

It is important to note that in certain jurisdictions, a family office may not be required to meet any specific requirements. However, besides the general compliance applicable to the type of entity that they use, certain family office services may trigger regulations and reporting obligations in different regions. Therefore, seeking advice from professionals in this area is necessary to ensure compliance and avoid legal issues.

5 Family offices and philanthropy

If you think you're too small to make a difference,

try spending the night with a mosquito.

African proverb

5.1 The strength of a family

Given their unique position as stewards of family wealth, family offices are in an excellent position to drive the adoption of more efficient practices in philanthropy.

In recent years, there has been a growing recognition that philanthropy can benefit from the same rigor and discipline as a business endeavor. This approach leverages the skills and expertise of family offices, which are often comprised of professionals with finance, law, and investment management backgrounds.

5.2 Having a business mindset to change

By applying a business mindset to philanthropy, family offices can maximize the impact of their resources. This involves setting clear goals and objectives and carefully monitoring progress against these objectives.

It may also include taking a more strategic approach to selecting charitable initiatives, focusing on those that align with the family's values, mission, and goals.

5.3 Greater impact

Family offices can drive greater efficiency and effectiveness by taking a more business-like approach to philanthropy. This, in turn, can help ensure that their charitable contributions significantly impact the causes they care about, creating a more sustainable and equitable world for all.

6 Common pitfalls

There are common pitfalls that might cause a split in the family office or create challenges.

When you marry a monkey for his wealth, the money goes,
but the monkey remains.
African proverb

6.1 The big D

Going through a divorce can be emotionally challenging and complex, which is why it is crucial to seek professional guidance to ensure you make informed decisions.

Seeking expert advice will help you understand the divorce outcomes and consider all matters involved, including lifestyle changes and financial decisions, to reach a fair settlement. Building wealth and securing a solid financial position can also help ensure individuals have better negotiating powers which often leads to a better settlement.

6.2 Mitigate undercurrents through initiative-taking planning

If advertising encourages people to live beyond their means,
so does matrimony.
Bruce Barton

Establishing governance structures, such as a Family Charter, to mitigate the impact of divorce on the family's overall wealth is essential. A Family Charter is a document that outlines the family's values, goals, and expectations. It can help prevent conflicts and provide a framework for decision-making.

6.3 High-profile divorce lawyers

Expert divorce lawyers can help navigate high-profile matters and provide valuable legal advice. Choosing the right team to assist you through the challenging moments is crucial, as they can provide you with the support and guidance you need to make informed decisions and protect your interests.

6.4 Don't fly solo

Successful families have unique needs, and collaborating with them requires tailored opportunities and services from professionals seeking to collaborate.

Given the family's vast resources and influence, understanding the family's needs is essential. Therefore, working with family offices requires highly personalized and bespoke solutions. If you try to do it on your own, you might fail.

6.5 Poor communication will show the cracks

Effective communication channels are critical in this sphere, as the dynamics of successful families often involve frequent changes in their affiliations. Maintaining confidentiality, transparency, and clarity is essential to ensure professional engagement.

If you don't do your paperwork, you will spend more time filling the gaps.

Multi-generational families take a structured approach, documenting their values and future vision by various methodologies. Seeking guidance from expert advisors is wise for anyone seeking to secure the longevity of a family's legacy.

6.6 Directors and officers (D&O) risks

Successful individuals are frequently invited to become independent directors of for-profit and non-profit organizations. The benefits of serving as a fiduciary can be numerous, including the opportunity to impact an organization's growth, expand a personal and professional network, and enhance one's experience.

Acting as a director, trustee or officer carries significant potential liability exposures. When considering a board role, family members should conduct due diligence and determine what level of coverage and indemnification the organization will provide.

The next step would be to consult with their risk advisor to determine whether the protections offered are adequate to satisfy their risk tolerance. One may want to add standalone D&O coverage to protect against potential exposures.

7 Continuous improvement

Not knowing where you stand and where you wish to be
will eventually create a tower moment.

Anne Klein

7.1 Gap analysis

Regularly reviewing a family office's current state is crucial to identifying operational gaps and risk factors and ensuring the office is on the right path toward sustainable wealth protection and transfer.

Defining and evaluating the in-house capabilities and employee roles is also important. Improving operations is vital for the family office's success, and creating a clear agenda and roadmap to execute these improvements is essential.

8 General practices for families

Three things in life—your health, your mission,
and the people you love. That's it.

Naval Ravikant

8.1 Get diving into the details

Intergenerational planning requires an in-depth analysis of each family-held asset and its holdings to guide the treatment and decision-making process for specific assets.

Owning an asset directly versus utilizing another usage model or holding structure is a significant consideration for family offices. *Succession planning* and empowering the family to succeed are critical elements for the sustainability of the legacy.

8.2 Do risk planning

Risk management is an essential aspect of running a family office. This covers standard risk factors, including insurance risk, reputational risk, cyber and physical security, financial risk and controls, and fraud prevention and detection.

Risk management must be a permanent feature of the family office agenda. Appointing a legal, risk, and compliance specialist can help guard against leaks.

8.3 Protection, preservation, and management

Preserving wealth continues to be a top concern.

Brian DeLucia

Family offices are critical in managing and preserving wealth for future generations. But it's not just about the numbers. Ethical considerations and integrity are paramount for decision-making when operating a family office. Ethical leadership sets the tone for the entire organization, inspiring and motivating everyone to uphold the highest standards of conduct.

8.4 External reporting

Family offices must grasp their reporting commitments and assess their existing reporting processes, roles, and accountabilities.

8.5 Flexibility for tax planning

Flexibility in how families invest, enjoy, utilize, and donate their wealth remains essential. With the added responsibility of ensuring they stay compliant with tax and exchange control regulations applicable, families who manage their wealth tax efficiently will have long-term benefits.

8.6 Ongoing review of worldwide tax position

Working with tax experts will assist families in analyzing their tax residency position and other tax obligations and strategies. Most countries have a residency tax basis; however, the United States, for example, has citizenship-based taxation. Understanding the tax implications of one's worldwide assets is essential.

8.7 Keeping matters in-house

Family offices possess the capacity to tailor their fundamental purpose and typically choose to retain certain aspects in-house.

These elements may include:

◆ Formulating their strategy.

◆ Implementing the strategy.

◆ Monitoring an investment policy statement.

◆ Strategic asset allocation.

- Manager selection.

- Benchmarking.

- Performance reporting.

- Due diligence.

- Tax planning and compliance.

- Succession and wealth transfer planning.

- Estate planning.

Nevertheless, other components may be outsourced or coexist within the family office environment.

8.8 Steer and control social media output

Social media utilization is crucial for family offices, and all family members, their advisors, and family office representatives must comprehend the family's social media requirements. This can be introduced via human resources policies, the family charter, and general training courses.

Appointing a public relations officer to monitor the family's social media presence can also help safeguard their privacy and reputation.

8.9 Keeping up with technology

We wanted to build technology that works for you,
not you working for your technology.

Domingo Viesca

Adopting technology can enhance the operational efficiency of the family office, and providers offer bespoke solutions specifically designed for family offices. Such solutions can range from consolidating global structures and holdings in a specific location to accounting tools and support systems, real estate maintenance, and more.

Family offices can achieve growth, stakeholder satisfaction, and retention through effective technology use.

8.10 Engaging with skilled people

The family office should also understand the bookkeeping and the role of the Chief Financial Officer (CFO).

This includes establishing the reporting framework, levels of responsibility, cash management oversight, budgeting processes, and forecasting analysis. Families sometimes outsource certain financial services, while others retain this function in-house.

8.11 Understand governance structures for growth

Family offices can help the family comprehend its requirements regarding family and business governance structures, training necessities for different family members, succession planning, and preserving the family's enterprising spirit.

8.12 Get access to data analytics and the intelligence you gather

Data analytics and management are neglected areas that require further exploration and will depend on the specific family office. Family offices should explore these areas, which should be addressed and can be crucial to ensuring their success. The family office should examine the specific data analytics and management tools that can aid their operations.

8.13 Dedicate time for continuity planning and strategic engagement

Successful families allocate time to grasp their family and business continuity plan, an ongoing process fundamental to elevating the family to the next level.

8.14 Focus on expansion and adoption

When families plan to expand globally, they must consider the impact of their international assets and businesses and deal with multi-jurisdictional operations and regulations. To minimize the risks associated with global expansion, families should seek specialized advice and ensure that an ultimate gatekeeper safeguards the advice they receive.

8.15 Mentor and mentee relationships for better results

Family offices provide an excellent platform for peer-to-peer discussions, allowing families to exchange shared experiences and find mentor/mentee prospects. These discussions can assist with scenario planning and create opportunities for building a safe network.

However, running a family office is not all about celebrating great wins. It requires an elevated level of dedication and care to manage the day-to-day running of a family office.

8.16 Family office networking

No level of technological sophistication can replace a handshake.
David Grammig

Build a solid network to create valuable connections, achieve objectives, and foster enduring relationships.

Though planning and occasional disengagement from your daily duties may be necessary, they can prove advantageous for your overarching goals. Prioritizing this aspect of your professional life can elevate your standing, provide a support system, and facilitate the development of subtle relationships. By building a solid network, you can ensure that your aspirations are realized in the long run.

8.17 Dynamic oversight

Family office employees should be ready to oversee the dynamic and mundane aspects of the job and deal with unexpected challenges that might arise.

8.18 Unpack and understand the reporting obligations

Family offices today face a significant challenge as they have a wide range responsibilities to fulfill. In addition, to preserving and growing family wealth, they must maintain and update financial records, monitor investment performance, ensure risk management, and maintain total tax and regulatory compliance. However, they are also committed to working collaboratively with other advisors and third-party service providers. This ensures that families have adequate liquidity to manage their obligations, as they are provided with consolidated reporting to give a clear and comprehensive view of their investments. Despite these challenges, family offices play a vital role in ensuring the financial well-being of families and their future generations.

9 A modern approach with a vintage touch

The fool speaks, and the wise man listens.
African proverb

9.1 Where wisdom and technology thrive

Families should consider utilizing social media platforms to promote their family office's activities, subject to understanding the risk factors.

9.2 Operational efficiency for longevity

Adopting technology can enhance the operational efficiency of the family office. Multiple providers offer *bespoke solutions* specifically designed for family offices, from consolidating global structures and holdings in a specific location to accounting tools and support systems, real estate maintenance, and more.

The family office should also clearly understand bookkeeping and the role of the CFO. This includes establishing the reporting framework, levels of responsibility, cash management oversight, budgeting processes, and forecasting analysis. Families can either outsource certain aspects of their financial services or retain this function in-house.

9.3 Dedicated investment policies

Specific investment policies or frameworks can help family offices stay on course and make informed decisions. Such frameworks assist with asset allocation, manager selection, benchmarking, performance reporting, and due diligence.

9.4 Governance structures

Family offices can also help the family comprehend its requirements regarding family and business governance structures, training necessities for different family members, succession planning, and preserving the family's enterprising spirit.

The modern family ...

> *The idea of "family first" is a powerful concept*
> *that suggests that when you prioritize your family,*
> *what you seek will naturally find its way to you.*
>
> Anne Klein

9.5 Alternative ways

Families are seeking alternative approaches to traditional monetary management. They want to feel more confident in their decisions and seek new ways to optimize their cash flows.

9.6 Focused alignment

Successful families prioritize aligning their interests to manage and optimize their cash flows. They also prioritize incorporating a true risk-adjusted philosophy that blends liquid and illiquid strategies while staying true to timeless values. This approach helps them achieve long-term growth and sustainability.

Family offices are not a sales platform; they keep the family tradition going through new *and* traditional methods. One of the competitive advantages of family offices is that they don't *sell products* or *endorse* service providers. Instead, they focus on aligning with other family offices, which positions them well for growth. This alignment means family offices can prioritize shared goals while staying true to their mission and values.

9.7 Reviving family goals

Intergenerational families must prioritize shared goals through alignment within their mission statement and shared values. This approach helps to ensure that everyone is working towards a common goal.

Families should also focus on surrounding themselves with talented people who can work together to bring collaborative endeavors to fruition for the greater good of others. By doing so, they can achieve tremendous success and impact.

10 Adding longevity to a family and individual story

My vision is for each one of us
to lead a rich and generous life.

Diana Chambers

Establish whether you need a family office or family-type services. Not all families require the support of a family office; however, those who can manage their wealth and business formally are more likely to achieve long-term success in this unique space.

Creating a successful family office necessitates a design with specific intentions and attention to several factors, such as family structures, asset holdings, ownership, and family capital.

While requirements may differ based on the family, business, and industry, essential components remain constant for all families, regardless of whether they operate within a family office framework.

It is critical to harmonize each element of the family and the family office while planning for unforeseen events, such as high-profile divorces, other life-changing events, or the exiting of family members, business associates, or family office personnel.

10.1 Identifying specific patterns to build on or to break it

Taking a higher perspective and analyzing situations without emotional attachment is crucial to identifying patterns and driving the family toward tremendous success. Professional engagements and family meetings are vital to maintaining authenticity and facilitating necessary conversations.

10.2 Find people with a good record

It is advisable to engage with specialized advisors to ensure the success of one's endeavors. These experts possess a wealth of experience and have encountered recurrent or similar scenarios. An outsider's perspective is often needed to identify gaps and misalignments between various stakeholders within the value chain.

Conflicting dynamics arise due to entrenched beliefs and missed opportunities; the actions and visions of the enterprise may need to align, thereby jeopardizing the growth and survival of the family office.

10.3 A portfolio of choice and variation

The family office ecosystem necessitates the availability of a comprehensive range of options for families and advisors to make informed decisions. As an advisor to a family, it is critical to establish ongoing communication with attorneys, accountants, family-specific advisors, family offices, and community asset owners.

Gathering intelligence and avoiding the flawed mentality of following the herd can help protect the family ecosystem by uncovering quantifiable scenarios.

10.4 Stay with the times while integrating solid principles

Each generation of a family has its unique focus when it comes to investments, including the use of Environmental, Social and Governance (ESG) compliant funds and socially responsible investments.

Some critical factors to consider when making investment decisions include:

◆ How investment strategies should be applied.

◆ How to approach distressed debt.

♦ How to use technology such as blockchain, digital assets, non fungible tokens, cryptocurrency, and tokenization.

Integrating each generation's different views and insights is crucial for a family office's survival. For instance, Generation Z might prioritize social impact and invest in technology integration.

10.5 On invitation only

Families and their representatives can access personalized services within the family office community. An engagement sheet is created based on the mutually agreed-upon principles of family office growth, which sparks the need for information and advice on best practices. It's important to note that each family has their distinct considerations.

10.6 Liquid and illiquid strategies

Successful families understand the importance of aligning their interests to manage and optimize their cash flows. They also prioritize incorporating a true risk-adjusted philosophy that blends liquid and illiquid strategies while staying true to timeless values.

This approach helps them achieve long-term growth and sustainability, essential for their family's well-being.

10.7 The power of decision-making

Family offices have a competitive edge because they do not sell products or endorse service providers. Instead, they concentrate on aligning with other family offices, which enables them to position themselves favorably for growth.

This alignment allows family offices to prioritize shared goals while remaining true to their mission and values.

10.8 No show and tell

Managing a family office is about more than just enjoying success. It demands a high level of commitment and attention to oversee the office's daily operations. Family office staff must be prepared to manage the job's dynamic and routine aspects and deal with unexpected challenges without making any billboard announcements.

It is advisable to exercise caution while utilizing social media platforms to promote family office activities.

A clear policy must be established, and all family members, their advisors, and family office representatives should work together to achieve their goals.

Confiding a secret to an unworthy person
is like carrying grain in a bag with a hole.

African Proverb

10.9 Stay in the know

Given the high volume of construction activity, investing in the multi-family space is a wise choice that requires reflection and alignment. With numerous projects underway, this sector could offer a promising opportunity for those seeking to create this type of portfolio.

11 Challenges in the family office ecosystem

Even the lion protects himself against flies.

African proverb

The individuals who possess the most wealth also hold the most noteworthy influence over how wealth is distributed. How wealth is applied and managed is constantly evolving. All vested parties must be willing to adapt by discovering innovative solutions and utilizing the methods and strategies that have enabled certain families and their advisors to become a formidable force in finance.

12 Complications in a family office

When two elephants fight, it is the grass that gets hurt.

African proverb

12.1 A chief without a tribe

The self-appointed "chief" typically causes a divide in the family. Executing essential decisions is more efficient if a proper governance structure exists. Strategies must be found to move past any embedded legacies that hold a negative connotation and stand in the way of the evolution of the family office.

13 Family office challenges

Family offices face a variety of specific challenges in different parts of the world.

Only a fool tests the depth of a river with no feet.

African proverb

13.1 The race is actual

Accessing talent is an ongoing challenge many countries face, particularly in affluent regions where specialized knowledge is critical in addressing local and global legislative and societal issues. Attempting to acquire and apply knowledge from foreign jurisdictions domestically can be disastrous.

This challenge is especially severe for families residing in countries where the development and enhancement of family wealth and enterprises should be prioritized. These countries require assistance in securing new opportunities and retaining growth opportunities for families.

This presents a significant challenge for families seeking alternative options to create wealth and establish family enterprises to sustain future generations.

13.2 Projecting future cross-border challenges

Scenario planning will assist families in exploring whether a family office is the preferred path to determining the family's future. A crucial discussion tool enabling families to make informed decisions is helping families understand any potential conflict situations that could harm their future success.

Mapping out the historical, current, and future scenarios, will aid understanding and help to unpack the tax realities and outcomes that may affect cash flow and other assets.

For instance, if family members reside in various parts of the world and use different structures to house wealth and business interests, some family members or assets could be adversely affected if initiative-taking planning is not done.

This could cause significant upsets, such as some family members needing to be willing to bear the tax expenses of a child who decides to be in a place where the tax system is more complex, which might result In higher tax regimes.

Families willing to deal with different scenarios to minimize the impact of disruptions and address how family members should be treated through their *Family Charter*, where they can agree on the principles of some issues, will ease into the next stage of their legacy story.

13.3 Countries with a futuristic view

Countries that prioritize the development of wealth and entrepreneurship tend to have a favorable attitude toward family wealth, family offices, and succession planning. In such countries, it is more acceptable to establish family office-led services as they align with their service models and enterprising spirit.

13.4 Focus on sophistication and not fluff

Countries must prioritize the development of specialized knowledge to tackle the challenge of limited access to skilled workers. Creating a supportive ecosystem that empowers families to establish and expand their businesses is crucial to providing sufficient resources and frameworks that offer growth opportunities for families and their wealth.

It will foster a favorable environment for developing family office-led services, enable families to access opportunities, and enhance their wealth and succession planning, thereby boosting the economy.

13.5 Resource requirements

What kind of resources are required for a family office to succeed? Write your own short list ...

---

14 Large family offices, where size does count

It always seems only possible once it's done.

Nelson Mandela

The United States of America remains the home to some of the most successful and well-known family offices. For instance, the founder of Walmart established a family office during his lifetime, which enabled his family to manage their assets, services, and philanthropic work with remarkable success.

Similarly, a family office based in other parts of the world for example, France holds significant value like the founder of L'Oréal.

New-age wealth creators are increasingly establishing family offices with substantial values and responsibilities.

Family offices are here to stay and will continue supporting the unique needs and visions of wealth creators and their families.

15 Define the decision-making process for greater impact

Yesterday, I was clever, and I wanted to change the world.
Today, I am wise, so I am changing myself.
Rumi

15.1 Participation in decisions or puppet-awareness strategies

To ensure the long-term success of a family office and effectively serve the interests of future generations, it is crucial to delineate the family's level of engagement in decision-making, establish unambiguous communication protocols, and formalize the management of family wealth. These elements are instrumental in optimizing the family office's operations and enhancing its efficacy.

Thoughtful deliberation and strategic planning are paramount in establishing a thriving family office that can adeptly cater to the family's requirements for generations to come.

15.2 Responsibility and decisions towards family wealth growth and protection

A wide range of professionals are available to assist, including experienced leaders in the family office environment. Services such as a Chief Financial Officer (CFO) can work in-house or be outsourced as well as in-house legal counsel or outsourced legal services, compliance and risk specialists, administrative personnel, and business development professionals.

16 Independence and interdependence of family offices

Understanding the independence and interdependence of the family office is crucial to families.

A family office can be an ideal solution for families who wish to maintain their independence and privacy from other families and service providers. It allows them to retain control over decision-making and establish a family service model that aligns with their value systems and identity.

This is particularly crucial for families who want to manage their wealth effectively while still receiving the support they need.

17 Intergenerational wealth transfers

Use family offices for intergenerational wealth transfers and gain access to experts.

All men have limits.
They learn what they are and learn not to exceed them.
I ignore mine.

Batman, Comics (Knightfall)

Intergenerational wealth is essential to many families' lives, and a family office can be an excellent tool for helping secure it. Contributing to societal change must also be considered. With the help of family offices, families can plan for their long-term success, ensuring that their legacy is preserved for future generations.

To establish and maintain an effective family office, it is imperative to have access to a team of experts who will help manage the family's wealth, legal matters, compliance, risk, and administrative and business development activities.

All stakeholders in the family office ecosystem should know their responsibilities regarding legal documentation, financial oversight, and reporting.

18 Industry establishment and branching out

Families with a long-standing history in a particular industry can use their knowledge and expertise to assist other businesses while staying within their expertise. However, some families may explore new industries and diversify their portfolios.

Despite this, they can still utilize their core values, leadership skills, and overall network to significantly impact a technical expert in a different sector. In such cases, having some level of control and economic benefits can be advantageous for the right family.

On the other hand, families that have accumulated wealth through non-operating businesses or inheritance may be better suited to partner with trusted managers recommended by their peers within the family office community.

18.1 Leadership styles

Leadership styles in family offices are subject to variation based on various factors, including regional disparities, organizational structures, cultural norms, and generational differences. In the United States, family offices tend to adopt professional management structures with clear hierarchies and reporting lines. The leadership is more centralized, focusing on financial expertise and investment strategies. The complex regulatory environment also promotes a culture of compliance and risk management, which, in turn, shapes leadership priorities.

Family office leadership is diverse in Europe, reflecting varying cultural norms in different countries. For instance, Switzerland emphasizes wealth preservation more than emerging markets.

In Asia, Confucian values have instilled a culture of respect for hierarchy and familial authority. Patriarchal or matriarchal leadership predominates, with decision-making centralized within the family. There is a growing shift towards institutionalization in dynamic economies such as Singapore and Hong Kong.

In Africa, family offices are mainly established based on the family culture and solutions are built around the family's needs.

18.2 Underlying forces

Single family offices (SFOs) are typically managed according to the preferences of the founding family. This can result in personalized and family-oriented leadership styles. However, as SFOs grow and become more complex, bringing in non-family executives to help manage the responsibilities may become necessary.

On the other hand, multi-family offices (MFOs) work with multiple families, each with unique interests and objectives. As a result, MFOs require skilled leadership that can balance these diverse interests. This requires solid relationship management skills to navigate potential conflicts and ensure operational efficiency while satisfying the needs of each client's family.

18.3 Generational forces at work

When it comes to family offices, there are often distinct differences between the leadership styles, perspectives, and characteristics of first-generation and second-generation leaders. These differences can be attributed to various factors, such as their experience, upbringing, exposure to wealth management, and how the wealth was created.

First-generation leaders responsible for founding or building the family office tend to have a robust entrepreneurial spirit. Their first-hand knowledge of business operations and investment strategies often makes them inclined to take a hands-on approach and actively participate in day-to-day operations. As the primary wealth creators, they tend to display a higher risk tolerance and greater autonomy in decision-making.

In contrast, second-generation leaders usually inherit wealth and may have a formal education in finance or related fields. They often prioritize wealth preservation over creation, adopting a more risk-averse or defensive stance and seeking input from various stakeholders in decision-making processes. To ensure long-term sustainability, they may introduce governance structures and succession plans.

Additionally, they often emphasize the importance of social impact and may incorporate impact investing and philanthropy into the family office's strategy to create positive social change alongside financial returns.

18.4 Impact Investing

Impact investing is experiencing ongoing growth and development, driven by a new generation of wealth owners seeking to create positive social and environmental change while achieving financial returns.

This dual goal is increasingly feasible due in part to regulatory measures, enhanced awareness of potential opportunities, greater consensus on effective practices, and the enabling role of technology.

Embarking on this journey may seem challenging, but navigating diverse generational dynamics, varying value sets, and numerous investment options presents an opportunity.

18.5 Cultural tones

Family offices are complex entities that require strong leadership to ensure success. However, the leadership style employed can vary significantly depending on the cultural nuances of the family in question. For example, in patriarchal societies, leadership may be centralized around one figure, while in more egalitarian cultures, collaborative decision-making is encouraged.

Moreover, some family offices also prioritize philanthropy and social responsibility, which can influence their leadership style. In such cases, leaders may prioritize impact investing and charitable initiatives aligning with broader societal goals and financial returns.

18.6 The custodians of the family wealth story

As custodians of a family's wealth and legacy, family office leaders are pivotal in determining their success both now and in the future. Effective leadership depends on understanding the family's values, navigating market dynamics, and complying with regulatory landscapes.

18.7 Family office leaders

Ultimately, a family office's achievements rest on the shoulders of its leaders. These leaders play a critical role in shaping objectives, making strategic decisions, and steering the overall trajectory of the family offices they serve. Some firms offer full-service resources and recruitment consultancy, working exclusively with family offices, to help those seeking expert support hire a leader who aligns seamlessly with their unique needs and values. Ideally, families should work with firms with a proven track record in executive search and a deep understanding of family office dynamics.

18.8 Mentoring within the family

Families who have a family office may want to identify talent from within their own family to participate in running it. They might want to mentor young family members to become leaders.

However, this must be done carefully, with clear guidelines and principles and a specific plan to empower the individual and help them understand the importance and responsibilities of the role.

It is essential to treat this with care, as it could be perceived as gaining access to more information than other family members or as a shift in dynamics by family office staff members.

Act and reflect on the following ...

The composition of your expert team:

The level of control:

What are the roles?

Are there any gaps?

List the service providers.

Are there any gaps?

What other resources do you require?

LDK — LDK

Reflecting on what I've read so far:

Chapter 4

Professional Services

Costs, Advisors, Specialities and Technology

I wouldn't say I like the phrase: Never cross a bridge till you come to it. The world is owned by men who cross bridges in their imaginations miles and miles before the procession.

Bruce Barton

Families require several phases to set up and design their family office, including evaluation, design, innovation, implementation, ongoing management and monitoring, and evolution.

Herewith a step-by-step approach to establish the needs of a family for expanded services. With this approach families can quickly determine where they are, where they wish to go, and how they see their future.

1 Family office set up and design

The foundation of starting a family office is by identifying the values of the family. It is important to understand what the family wishes to accomplish through the creation of a family office.

Create a clear picture of your current situation

Consider the support, services, and advice your business and outside advisors provide for family members, including, but not limited to, income tax compliance, investment planning, property management, asset protection, administration support, and investment strategies.

Families can integrate these services into the family office and prioritize them by complexity, importance, and risk.

Evaluate the complexity of family, wealth, and business

Consider the size of a family, the generational reach, the number of legal entities, the type of assets, and any inter-family transactions that might exist. Families must determine if managing their wealth requires the organized structure of a family office.

Determine your intergenerational goals

When life and business become more complex, the services required from a family office should match these complexities. Therefore, it is important to develop a future-state strategy for the family's life, and the family office must be in line with the family goals.

Analyze your advisory teams, the coordination of their advice, and the cost elements

Family offices streamline the process of having numerous advisors for different aspects of the family's wealth management. To understand the current cost element better, calculate the current costs paid for financial advice, legal counsel, tax planning, estate planning, and asset management.

Compare this with the potential costs of setting up and operating a family office.

Determine the family's specific needs

Are there any confidentiality or security needs or concerns? If privacy is paramount, a single family office may be more attractive. Families need to understand what they wish to control and retain in-house.

Decide on the level of control the family would like to retain

If a family wishes to direct how specific tasks are conducted, they will need oversight of individual activities. In other situations, the family's desires will determine how a third-party vendor provides services but not control their execution.

Reputation and risk management

The fundamental aim of most family offices is to mitigate potential loss and damage to the family, whether financial, physical, or reputational. Such risks can originate from various sources, including business operations, investments, technology, or other operational factors. It is essential to ascertain the assistance required to manage compliance, risk, and reputational issues. Failure to comply with governing regulations can result in significant monetary loss and reputational harm, making it imperative to understand the potential consequences.

2 The role of founders and their operations

The role of a founder in a growing company can be challenging when it comes to managing it effectively. Therefore, it is crucial to consider the best approach to transition from founder to Chief Executive Officer (CEO). There are two options: hiring a CEO, or selling a controlling interest to a family or private equity firm that will hire a CEO.

While it is true that keeping the founder as CEO and hiring a Chief Operating Officer (COO) can create confusion and tension, every situation is unique, and there may be circumstances where it could work. However, it is worth evaluating the potential risks and benefits before deciding.

2.1 What is the role of the founder moving forward?

The role of the founder in an organization is often seen as one that should maintain distance from operational tasks. It is equally essential for them to remain engaged in preserving the company's distinct culture and ensuring its vision is on track. This is what sets a business apart from others. Unfortunately, companies lose their identity and direction when the founder is relegated to the background and kept out of sight, resulting in a sterile atmosphere.

3 Barriers in the absence of wealth structures

There are key barriers that a family might have to overcome should they not have any wealth structures.

3.1 Where does one start?

Start with the basics, with an end goal in mind, and have a plan. This strategic approach provides a clear path forward and instills a sense of security, knowing you are prepared for any challenges.

3.2 Perceived and natural barriers that can deplete value

Many people experience fear and uncertainty when they don't know what to do or where to turn for help. This can be particularly challenging when facing difficult situations such as illness, financial problems, or family issues. Additionally, denial of the realities and the future can prevent individuals from acting and seeking necessary support. In some cases, the wider family may also struggle with the inaccessibility of information, which can be a significant barrier to getting the help they need.

Finally, a lack of knowledge and understanding about available resources and support can make it difficult for the wider family to provide practical assistance and guidance.

4 Local connections, international networks, global expansion

Customize the advisory board ...

Advisors from around the world work together to provide services to wealthy families. Each country faces unique challenges and has a distinct culture, which is essential to consider when setting up a family office.

When affluent families expand their businesses globally or to a specific jurisdiction, aligning local expertise with global networks is essential due to their family and business dynamics. In the United States of America, advisors have access to a vast network of global single- and multi-family office communities, commonly known as *family offices*. Other countries may be at different stages of development.

As wealth expands and moves worldwide, specialized expertise is required to support this expansion.

5 Service provider selection risk

A family office, should consider outsourcing some of their operations and investment team decisions to the right service providers, at the right price. To do this, one must first create a family office compass, which involves understanding where the family is headed and what the family office's mission is.

It is crucial to have an experienced and well-connected advisory board to review the most qualified service providers. This way, families can avoid selecting service providers based on location, personal connections, or familiarity, thereby ensuring service providers are in alignment with family values.

6 Operational costs and other considerations

Operational costs are unavoidable and should be considered when establishing a family office. A range of factors must be considered, such as the cost of implementing systems and the expense of outsourcing certain functions.

Upskilling and finding talented staff are crucial ecosystem components that should be noticed.

7 Family Office professional networks and culture

Quality is not an act; it is a habit.
Aristotle

7.1 Don't just let anyone in — *check them out first!*

The family office society is an informal, private network that safeguards the family story and privacy. Advisors within this community have close personal relationships that set them apart from others and make them well-respected.

Advisors who work with families know how to communicate on specific platforms and have private conversations about family wealth to maintain a professional environment. Family offices prefer to interact with like-minded people and prioritize people first.

By participating in closed networks, advisors gain access to limited resources, attend founder-led fireside chats and industry events, and improve the industry's dynamics.

7.2 Long-term engagement

Excellent care and diligence are essential when working with families spanning multiple generations. Advisors must adhere to legislative requirements and document everything to understand the family's story and take appropriate action fully.

Regarding family offices, no single approach works for everyone when choosing between direct and manager selection. Because the industry is not straightforward, each family office is unique.

7.3 Shared commonalities

Every family has a unique set of financial needs. Each family office requires a customized approach that caters to their specific requirements.

However, despite these differences, families share commonalities regarding various areas of their wealth cycles.

These areas may include:

- Budgeting.

- Investment planning.

- Risk management.

- Tax planning.

- Estate planning.

- Philanthropy.

Understanding these shared areas can help family offices create a tailored approach that meets their client's needs and helps them achieve their financial goals.

7.4 Skilled people unlock professional culture

One thing is sure in an uncertain world: Family offices require skilled resources and dedication to actively reflect on the family wealth ecosystem, trading entities, and the family's well-being. The advisory teams' careful selection and due diligence should drive the family office, where skills, goals, and culture should align.

7.5 Compliance matters

Don't think there are no crocodiles just because the water is calm.

African Proverb

Acquiring counsel from other legal domains is imperative, encompassing compliance matters, tax implications, and general commercial principles.

Compliance matters are important as they refer to the regulations and rules that must be observed to operate a family office lawfully. Tax implications are paramount, as they can significantly impact the family office's financial operations.

Finally, understanding and complying with general commercial principles is essential to ensuring that the family office operates according to standard business practices.

It is imperative to seek counsel from experts in these various legal domains to ensure the family office's smooth and lawful operation.

Private companies — the role of the company secretary

Building a business and creating wealth requires a host of services and support. One element is ensuring you have company secretarial services in place.

8 The family office realities

> *It's tough to get out of bed to do roadwork at 5 am*
> *when you've been sleeping in silk pajamas.*
> Marvin Hagler

8.1 Deep expertise and generalist support

To make well-informed decisions about acquiring assets or business interests, family offices must seek the advice of experts in the field. These experts may include financial advisors, lawyers, and other professionals with the knowledge and experience to provide valuable insights and guidance.

A collaborative approach between family offices and these professionals can facilitate the development of a comprehensive strategy tailored to meet the unique needs and goals of the family office.

By carefully considering the advice of these professionals, family offices can make strategic investments that align with their long-term objectives and lead to sustainable growth and prosperity.

8.2 Culture is king — challenging work is a reality

Each family and advisor will have a unique approach, and each family office will have its distinct feel and culture. While these elements can help resolve issues, they can add to the complexities.

Founders and executives who actively engage with these aspects may prevent defeats regarding time wastage, missed opportunities, and losses in monetary value.

8.3 For the love of the game

Any advisor who wants to work in this environment will know that it required dedication and hard work.

Success in the family office requires **long-term commitment**, but gives peace of mind if both the family and advisors are enthusiastic about making a difference.

9 A view from above

It's better to be an optimist who is sometimes wrong than a pessimist who is always right.

Mark Twain

Focusing on the big picture and small actions is essential to shaping a family office's future.

Critical discussions and healthy partnerships can help promote sustainability and inclusion with guidance and support from experts within the family office community.

9.1 Action in motion

Taking an initiative-taking approach that spans different dimensions is necessary to support a family office's evolution and day-to-day operations. This approach should cover diverse topics, including generational matters, various territories, and multi-layered issues.

The complexity of family office operations and family businesses demands solid resources that are critical drivers to success. These resources should Range from the human element, based on trusted relationships, to the technological side, which enhances efficiency.

9.2 Professional element

An effective family office can access a variety of experts who can help manage the family's wealth, legal matters, compliance, risk, and administrative and business development activities. The resources required for a family office may vary depending on the type of family office used.

One main priority should be establishing a plan for how family wealth can be managed more effectively. To do this, it is essential to have access to a range of professionals, including:

♦ Leaders in the family office environment.

♦ A Chief Financial Officer (CFO), who can be either in-house or outsourced.

♦ In-house legal counsel or outsourced legal services.

- Compliance and risk specialists.

- Administrative personnel.

- Business development experts.

Individual support for family members

Some families ensure fairness by appointing a key advisor for each family member. The fundamental relationship person has a critical role and is appointed to function as a communication conduit and assist with significant decisions and choices for the family and the individual.

Discussions may also encourage legacy-building techniques among younger family members, such as creating a junior or shadow board or involving them in family philanthropy.

10 Effective advisory boards and professional support

Family office "advice is often like gas station sushi ...
there's something not right"

Michael Foster

The continuous rise in family offices, where the global assets now exceed US$7 trillion, requires solid advisory and structuring support. An effective advisory board should include both family and non-family members, with family representatives equipped to oversee governance-related issues when needed.

Expert advice

It is vital to seek professional advice from specialists who can explain the laws and regulations that apply to family offices and their services. By doing so, family offices can operate compliantly and efficiently while avoiding legal issues.

Industry experts

Many operating businesses, including family office organizations, have a group of trusted advisors from related industries who provide valuable insights and advice.

The more a family office focuses on building a diverse and robust board of Advisors, the greater the benefits they will receive from having access to such a resource.

Family office experts

Several factors should be considered when selecting a family office expert. A proven record in managing family offices and experience dealing with similar clients will be of terrific value. Ensure they offer support services that align with your family's needs, from investment management to estate planning.

Families should choose experts who provide customized solutions rather than a one-size-fits-all service, as every family office has unique requirements. Ensure the consultant meets the highest ethical standards and complies with all relevant regulations.

Chief Financial Officer (CFO)

The resources required for a family office depend on the type of family office being used. A crucial aspect is establishing and mapping how family wealth can be institutionalized.

To achieve this, it is essential to have access to a range of professionals, including leaders in the family office environment, a CFO who can either be in-house or outsourced, in-house legal counsel or outsourced legal services, compliance and risk specialists, administrative personnel, and business development experts.

Family preferences for keeping the CFO in-house

For most families, having an in-house CFO who can expertly manage wealth, legal counsel who can oversee legal matters discreetly and efficiently, and compliance and risk specialists who can identify and mitigate potential risks is imperative.

Most families prefer this approach, which can help ensure that their financial and legal matters are overseen professionally and securely.

Outsource the Chief Investment Officer (CIO) and other functions

The hiring of outsourced CIOs is growing and will continue as more family offices are started daily. Existing family offices seek to expand their investing activities and formalize their portfolio management. The CIO must be aligned to the values and the best interest of the family.

Trust services and specialists

Wealth could last much longer if the assets are held in a trust structure, where sophisticated trustees can oversee the wealth, preserve, and grow it, and support the beneficiaries.

Specialist advice is required from the start of the planning phase to the final stage of the journey.

Public Relations Officers

A public relations officer can assist with maintaining the family's reputation and ensuring the family uses social media platforms responsibly, minimizing potential reputational risk and economic losses.

Business Development and support personnel

It is imperative to have the expertise of competent business development professionals and administrative personnel to ensure the seamless operation of a family office and to successfully identify investment opportunities that align with the family's objectives.

Professional counsel

Families can achieve their goals and strengthen their legacy over the long, medium, and short term by seeking professional resources. Many families have successfully implemented this strategy over multiple generations, and it can be the key to sustained success. By working closely with professionals, families can ensure the smooth running of their affairs, define mandates and goals, and minimize delays.

Careful consideration of legal work, contractual oversight, and steps to be taken in case of litigation will ensure that daily operations run smoothly. Regulatory requirements and the parties responsible for compliance and ownership should also be considered.

By taking these steps, families can set themselves up for success and achieve their goals.

11 What makes the perfect family office legal counsel?

11.1 Critical role

Family offices play a critical role in managing the wealth of high-net-worth families, and as such, they must navigate a broad range of complex legal issues. Like other businesses and organizations, family offices require the guidance of legal counsel who can provide sound advice and assistance.

However, due to the unique nature of family politics and succession concerns, family office legal counsel must give strategic guidance and be a cultural fit to address these intricate issues effectively.

11.2 Trusted advisor

Family office legal counsel is a trusted advisor with the expertise required to address legal issues and understand the complex dynamics of the family and its business. As such, their responsibilities go beyond traditional legal advice, and they must provide strategic guidance that aligns with the family's long-term goals and objectives.

The role of family office legal counsel is critical to the success of high-net-worth families. They must navigate complex legal issues while considering the family's unique dynamics and succession concerns.

By providing sound legal and strategic guidance, they ensure that the family's wealth is protected and grows over time.

The role of the legal advisor

The role of a legal advisor in a family office involves more than just the usual legal advisory duties. They must deal with diverse asset portfolios and multiple legal and regulatory matters.

Their responsibilities include estate planning, tax liabilities, trust administration, company secretarial duties, and compliance oversight.

Adaptability

It's important to note that this role requires adaptability, as it can vary significantly depending on the specific needs and structure of the family office. Given the familial politics involved, a legal counsel may also need to help resolve complex or sensitive family disputes in addition to their usual duties.

11.3 What do family offices seek in key appointments?

Family offices prioritize a combination of personality traits, experience, and cultural fit when hiring key staff members. The ideal candidate must possess strong interpersonal skills, proficiency in communication, and extensive legal expertise and skill set.

They must be able to navigate complex family relationships, deal with succession planning and intergenerational wealth transfer, explain complex matters clearly and understandably, and provide personalized and tailored solutions to address the family's unique circumstances and objectives.

Due to the amount of sensitive information involved, the highest level of confidentiality and discretion is expected.

Hiring considerations

When hiring a family office, several factors require careful consideration. Ensuring the candidate's alignment with the family's values and long-term objectives is crucial. A proactive attitude in strategic decision-making and a willingness to assume increasing responsibilities is necessary. Reputation matters significantly in the legal field, so a strong track record of success and integrity is essential.

A broad network is required, as they often must collaborate with other professionals, such as financial advisors, accountants, and investment managers. Prior experience working with ultra-high-net-worth individuals or family offices offers a better understanding of the industry and the ability to navigate complex family dynamics.

Let's work together to build a society where people come first,

and positive behaviors and outcomes

are the foundation of governance.

Brian DeLucia

To make informed decisions, family offices must seek the guidance of experts in various fields. Working alongside financial advisors, lawyers, and other specialists can help develop a comprehensive strategy tailored to meet a family office's unique needs and goals.

A proactive approach towards culture and engagement

can prevent losses and missed opportunities.

Accessing various resources supporting the family office's day-to-day operations and evolution is essential, from human resources to technological advancements.

Effective advisory boards and professional support can provide valuable insights and advice while ensuring compliance with laws and regulations.

Selecting a family office expert with a proven track record in managing family offices and experience dealing with similar clients is crucial. It is of the utmost importance to choose experts who provide customized solutions that meet the unique requirements of each family office.

11.4 Global effective tax rate planning

A competitive tax regime is often considered a key factor in a Family Office's evaluation process to decide where to shop.

With the introduction of the new Capital Investment Entrant Scheme (CIES), tax concessions for Family-owned Investment Holding Vehicles (FIHVs), market facilitation measures, and the establishment of the Network of Family Office Service Providers, we have witnessed a sharp increase in interest and inquiries from ultra-high net worth (UHNW) individuals and families considering the establishment of Family Offices in Hong Kong.

Anthony Lau

In today's global marketplace, families and advisors must anticipate and understand tax planning decisions' potential short- and long-term consequences. This must be done at a coordinated, worldwide level and in the context of the family and the broader business objectives.

International tax professionals can help families navigate the complexities of multiple tax systems and international regulations worldwide.

Various international tax planning, consulting, and compliance services are available, ranging from those just beginning to invest internationally to large multinationals.

11.5 Philanthropy experts

***Philanthropy is a means of doing good and helping others
and is a powerful tool in a family office's investment strategy.***

Simple, insight, family office.

Aside from the drive and passion that motivates philanthropy, there are various paths to take, and seeking expert advice is crucial when families determine their Involvement in philanthropy.

Matters such as climate change, biodiversity, health, education, and other philanthropic objectives and aspirations require professional guidance and support.

11.6 Governance, risk, and compliance

Risk management and compliance are two vital pillars for family offices. They need to sustain growth, preserve wealth, and maintain the trust of the family and stakeholders. Implementing proper risk management and compliance measures is a reactive and initiative-taking strategy to secure the family's legacy.

To enhance the efficiency and effectiveness of their decision-making process, family offices are strongly recommended to adopt an initiative-taking, holistic, and adaptable approach incorporating risk management and compliance as integral components. This approach is essential for ensuring that family offices can keep pace with the constantly evolving regulatory landscape and effectively manage the diverse risks they may encounter.

By adopting this approach, family offices can achieve a heightened level of preparedness that enables them to navigate the challenges of the modern business environment with greater ease and confidence.

Investment committees

Family offices typically have various committees to manage their investment portfolios. For example, they may establish a *Strategic Investments Committee* and a *Tactical Committee* to adjust quickly to changes in the macro-economic environment.

An influential *Investment Committee* should operate within a clearly defined investment policy that specifies the investment goals, risk tolerance, asset allocation, and how it will oversee its investments. This policy should serve as a guiding document for investment-related decisions.

11.7 Lifestyle support

A family office can opt for extensive private services catering to their personal assistance needs. These services can be sourced through a network of trusted providers, including various concierge services. The service will depend on the family's preferences and needs.

Health ...

I love the philosophy of earmarking capital for families and healthcare for their children.

Brian DeLucia

11.8 Divorce has an impact on the family office and the family

Obtain divorce concierge services and general planning for greater peace of mind.

Older women who experience a divorce see their standard of living decline by 45%. That is much more severe than for men, who see a drop of 21%.

When contemplating a divorce or when confronted by the realities of a divorce, consider collaborating with professionals who understand the impact of divorce on the family wealth business structures and the family office.

Besides the emotional turmoil, divorce remains challenging to navigate for all parties. Having the correct professionals by your side and using your intuition will guard you against challenging financial outcomes.

What remains essential before one enters a marital regime is to understand the government, the legal principles, and the possible outcome of death or divorce. **Get independent advice from an expert.**

While divorce is a reality, it is advisable to understand the impact of various scenarios; for example, is it possible to have a "clean" break, what structures will be held intact or created, and how will this impact your ability to live a life of independence away from the marriage that ended?

There are ways in which a settlement can be reached Where all matters are considered, such as lifestyle changes, financial and practical decisions, and their impact.

Planning for fairness

At the same time, one can create wealth and ensure that throughout the marriage, one focuses on securing one's wealth by placing oneself in a better financial position and having stronger negotiating powers. Marriage and divorce planning elements can also be incorporated into the *Family Charter.*

11.9 Lifestyle management and concierge services

Family Offices offer more than just financial and governance services. They can also provide a wide range of personalized lifestyle management and concierge services to cater to family member's specific needs and preferences.

These services are designed to improve quality of life and provide individualized care. Integrating lifestyle management and concierge services into the family office's offerings brings numerous advantages and challenges, enhancing the overall value proposition for family members and adding another layer of responsibility to the office.

It demands a different level of commitment and must find alignment within the family office's framework.

Some of these services may include:

Art and collections management: Curating and supervising valuable art collections, antiquities, and other assets.

Culinary experiences: Coordinating private chefs, culinary classes, wine-tasting sessions, and making reservations at esteemed restaurants.

Education support: Assisting in the selection of educational institutions, provision of tutors, arranging specialized academic programs, and managing educational trusts.

Entertainment and leisure coordination: Arranging tickets for concerts, theaters, sporting events, or exclusive private entertainment experiences.

Event planning: It involves ensuring detailed arrangements for personal or family events such as weddings, anniversaries, birthdays, and other celebrations.

Health and wellness: Coordinating healthcare needs such as regular check-ups, specialist consultations, dietary guidance, and rejuvenating retreats focused on well-being.

Household management: Recruiting and supervising domestic staff, managing household finances, and coordinating day-to-day household activities.

Travel coordination: Organizing personal or family vacations, business trips, and immersive travel experiences.

Real estate management: Supervising the maintenance, refurbishment, acquisition, or sale of residential or commercial properties.

Personalized assistance: Offering comprehensive support for various tasks and activities as a personal assistant to family members.

Personal shopping and styling: Provide personal shoppers or stylists to assist in procuring clothing, gifts, or other personal items.

Transportation services: Manage private vehicles and drivers and arrange luxurious transportation as needed.

Personalized communication: Handling personal correspondence, invitations, thank-you notes, and other communication needs.

Integrating style management and concierge services into the family office's offerings presents numerous advantages, enhancing the overall value proposition.

11.10 Best-in-class associations

Building relationships with top-notch service providers within a family office can create a formidable team of support professionals that can help with various roles, such as:

♦ Board structure.

- Philanthropy planning.

- Venture investing.

- Business advisory services.

- Legacy and next-generation support and planning.

- Transition or succession planning.

- Structural review and restructuring.

- Use of private trust company structures.

- Different models for the family office.

- Identifying missing links and opportunities.

- Non-financial services selection and review.

- Identifying family talent and providing support on how to retain and enhance it.

- Reviewing non-core and core businesses.

- Family and advisor protocol model.

- Family office investment introductions.

- Environmental, social, and governance (ESG) strategies and measurements.

- Training and knowledge-sharing best practices.

- Brand building for the family.

- Private lending scenarios.

- Gaining access to the insider world of private lending.

- Total balance sheet opportunities.

- Maximizing opportunities.

- Niche discussions and introductions.

- Private dinners.

- Strategic conversations.

- Transactional experience and support and tracking.

- Knowledge of systems reviews.

- System support and maintenance.

- Physical security training and review of service providers.

- Cybersecurity awareness and protection.

- Conflict resolution and policies.

- Lifestyle design and management.

- Tax structure network.

- Private equity networks regulatory and reporting obligations.

- Consolidated reporting across geographies, asset classes, total circle views, and specific legal services insights.

12 Best in class service

Family offices provide highly personalized services tailored to each family member's unique preferences and needs. To achieve this, the office endeavors to understand each family member's goals, values, and interests. They offer a comprehensive suite of services that simplify coordination and assist decision-making by providing a single point of contact for various services, reducing the family's administrative burden.

Quality control is fundamental in ensuring all services meet the highest standards and align with the family's values. The family office conducts rigorous due diligence on all service providers, such as investment managers, lawyers, and accountants, to ensure they meet the highest standards of professionalism, ethics, and expertise.

One of the primary benefits of utilizing a family office is the time it saves for family members to focus on their core business and personal affairs. The family office support structure relieves family members from mundane or time-consuming tasks, allowing them to focus on their interests and pursuits.

The family office handles all administrative tasks, such as managing household staff, paying bills, and managing properties.

Discretion and privacy are of the utmost importance in a family office. The office recognizes that confidentiality is paramount and that the family's affairs should always be confidential. They handle all matters with the highest level of confidentiality, respecting the family's privacy.

In summary, a family office is a dedicated and personalized service that understands each family member's unique needs and preferences. They provide a comprehensive suite of services that simplify coordination, assist decision-making, and save family members' time.

The office operates with the highest quality control standards, ensuring that all services meet the highest standards and align with the family's values. Lastly, they deal with all matters with the utmost discretion and confidentiality, respecting the family's privacy.

13 The use of technology to enhance efficiency

Build something that outlives you.

Anonymous

13.1 Find the right fit

Various technological systems can improve family offices' efficiency and management. These systems provide a comprehensive platform that includes multiple components, which can be used to get an overview of the family's financial status, asset holdings, ownership structures, and more.

13.2 Improve communication

One of the most critical components of a family office is communication. A dedicated communication system can be implemented to ensure that communication channels are easy and seamless among family members and their advisors. This system can enable fast and secure messaging, video conferencing, and other communication methods, allowing for better collaboration and decision-making.

13.3 Asset management

In addition to communication, independent systems can be used for specific types of asset management, such as real estate systems. These systems can provide a detailed analysis of real estate holdings, including rental income, lease agreements, and maintenance costs.

13.4 Meeting facilitation

Family offices can utilize various systems, such as family meeting facilitation support systems, anti-money laundering systems, and know-your-client systems.

13.5 Systems review and procurement

When acquiring these systems, it is important to conduct careful procurement and analysis to ensure they meet the family office's specific needs. Moreover, it is essential to protect sensitive information by implementing robust security measures to prevent unauthorized access or data breaches.

Technological systems can provide family offices with a more efficient and streamlined approach to management, improving their financial standing and overall performance.

13.6 Estate Planning

Estate planning is a crucial process encompassing several steps to achieve the desired outcomes. Various factors, such as personal, family, and business interests, must be considered when creating an estate plan for each family member.

Outlined below are some action steps that can assist in getting started:

♦   Draft estate planning documents with the help of an expert panel.

♦   Check registration requirements and seek assistance if needed.

♦   Understanding the tax implications and consequences of transferring assets into a structure.

♦   Identifying professionals who can help with the administration of structures and investments.

♦   Determining the duties and powers of professionals and the authorization required.

♦   Review the structure periodically and make changes, as necessary.

♦   Keeping up with legislative changes and exploring other markets or jurisdictions if needed.

♦   Considering exploring philanthropic goals as part of the estate plan.

As it develops, ensuring that the estate plan aligns with the growth strategy and succession plan is crucial. These steps can help create a comprehensive estate plan that meets the desired needs and objectives.

13.7 Enduring fundamentals for estate planning

The foundation of estate planning involves several factors, such as family harmony, tax planning, liquidity, retirement provision, asset protection, and feasibility.

A well-crafted *estate plan* should help in the smooth administration of assets, safeguard business interests, ensure continuity, provide for employees, ensure liquidity, maintain control, and allow flexibility. Several estate planning strategies include legal vehicles such as companies, trusts, foundations, buy and sell agreements, and assurance policies.

13.8 Estate planning for people in blended families

I have gained a unique perspective on life through my personal experiences with family illness, the death of loved ones, and divorce within my inner and professional circles. When we approach situations with compassion, understanding, and careful planning, we value strong relationships and understand the importance of navigating toxic ones. Our insights can assist others facing challenges impacting their wealth and personal well-being. Ultimately, everything starts with self-compassion.

Anne Klein

The estate planning process can be complex, especially involving blended-family couples and partners. This demographic often encounters unique challenges that differ from those of single-relationship couples.

Estate planning techniques that work well for the latter may only be suitable for the former with significant modification, making it crucial to exercise caution and attention to detail in planning an estate for blended families. This is particularly important for individuals who have experienced divorces, remarriages, and blended family situations, as they know the complexities involved.

In conclusion, it is crucial to recognize the significance of estate planning for blended families and to take the necessary steps to ensure that this process is approached with the utmost care and attention to detail. In this way, individuals can be confident that their assets will be distributed according to their wishes and that their loved ones will be protected.

13.9 Letter of wishes

We all want to ensure that our loved ones are cared for
even when we're no longer around.

Brian DeLucia

Writing a wish letter is one way to ensure our feelings are known. A letter of wishes is a powerful tool that enables us to communicate our final wishes clearly and concisely. This letter can express one's desires regarding assets, trusts, and personal affairs.

By writing down these wishes, one can ensure that loved ones know exactly what we want to achieve, in a non-binding manner.

Additionally, a letter of wishes can help minimize potential conflicts and disputes among family members or other interested parties. Through these clear and specific instructions, we can reduce the chances of misunderstandings and ensure that everyone is on the same page.

A letter of wishes is a document that guides those managing your estate or family trust on how you want your assets to be dealt with. Unlike a will, a letter of wishes is **not legally binding**, and fiduciaries are not obliged to follow any requests made in the letter.

Therefore, to ensure that specific personal possessions go to particular beneficiaries, including them in your will is better option.

A letter of wishes can't replace a will, but it can provide practical and emotional support to your executors, family members, and trustees created in the will.

13.10 The importance of having a last will and testament

Speaking to experts about one's will or multiple wills is crucial. This requires unpacking your marital regime, relationship status, family, business, and asset structure. It will assist you in determining the impact of having assets in different locations, or if you are a multinational, consider having an additional will and ensure that there is at least one will that covers all other jurisdictions not covered in a specific will.

The effect of tax on your estate will also be explained, as will the family's estate planning strategies. Any taxes and the impact of taxes on death should also be unpacked. Multiple wills must be coordinated to ensure one will does not supersede the other.

13.11 The complexities of estate planning and international wealth planning

Always surround yourself with experts with a global reach and an understanding of local topics. Always search for the best advice, and don't hesitate to ask questions. Seek an answer with which you are comfortable. See different advisors, look for independent support, and take steps to implement any solid solutions suggested to you. In my experience, obtaining a written legal opinion that can be kept on file not only acts as a form of protection but also highlights areas that need attention. A legal opinion is not set in stone; it is simply an opinion based on certain principles and the author's understanding, the legal position, the factual information shared, and a few other factors. Some matters are grey, while others are black and white. Get a good lawyer, and you'll see the difference. Know when to get updated advice and let go of certain strategies. Always protect your integrity.

Anne Klein

14 Digital assets

Digital assets are not just complex and multifaceted, they are also the gateway to our lives and legacies. This makes a thorough appraisal of one's digital footprint a necessity. Families should recognize the urgency of safeguarding their digital legacy, as it has significant implications for both personal and professional contexts.

In this age of rapid digital transformation, a comprehensive understanding of digital assets and their management is important, and it is indispensable.

15 Social engineering

Cybercriminals use various tactics to defraud victims. For instance, they may use personal or professional information to appear credible and deceive individuals into willingly disclosing sensitive information or transferring money electronically.

Social engineering attacks can be simple phishing emails, which aim to trick recipients into clicking malicious links, or more sophisticated schemes involving impersonation through fake phone calls and emails. One such scheme, business email compromise (BEC), consists of impersonating a trusted contact to persuade employees to wire funds for a supposed business transaction.

16 Family offices: Client Relationship Management (CRM)

16.1 Purpose, passion, and service

Client relationship management (CRM) is a fundamental aspect of the intricate and highly individualized sphere of family office services. Whether dealing with single family offices (SFOs) or multi-family offices (MFOs), establishing and perpetuating robust client relationships is paramount. This requires a comprehensive grasp of family members' distinctive needs, objectives, preferences, and values, along with providing a consistent, high-caliber service experience.

Multiple pivotal components of client relationship management are prevalent in both SFOs and MFOs. These encompass a thorough comprehension of clients' requisites and goals, the creation of customized service frameworks, regular communication and reporting maintenance, utilization of contemporary technology, and adherence to relevant legislation and regulations while ensuring confidentiality.

Discrepancies exist in the implementation of CRM practices between SFOs and MFOs. SFOs typically nurture more intimate and customized relationships, whereas MFOs may adhere to a more formal and standardized yet highly personalized approach. Addressing the needs and expectations of numerous families can introduce complexity.

16.2 Challenges in CRM

Challenges in client relationship management (CRM) within family offices encompass the management of clients' expectations, reconciling generational dissimilarities, guaranteeing data security, and resolving conflicts. To surmount these challenges, CRM best practices include the routine assessment and updating of client profiles, development of communication strategies, investment in training and development, integration of technological solutions, and evaluation of client contentment.

The CRM landscape within family offices is anticipated to comprise more sophisticated utilization of AI and automation to elevate personalized service, more comprehensive family involvement, and virtual engagement as notable attributes of client relationships. In summary, CRM embodies a multifaceted and pivotal constituent of family office services, mandating an in-depth comprehension of clients, a personalized approach, durable communication strategies, and perpetual adjustment to evolving requisites and technologies.

16.3 Common traps related to family offices

There are common traps that should be avoided when dealing with family offices.

Family offices are complex

Advisors working for family offices must be aware of potential problems that can harm their operations and relationships with the families they serve. Each family has unique needs, preferences, and values, and a one-sided approach to service offerings may not be practical. Personalizing and customizing service delivery to meet each family's specific needs is essential. Advisors need to take the time to understand the family's financial goals, risk tolerance, and legacy planning requirements.

Compliance

Compliance with regulations is not only a legal requirement but also an indicator of the family office's professionalism and credibility. Ignoring or overlooking regulatory requirements can lead to legal repercussions, financial penalties, and a damaged reputation.

Advisors working for family offices must be updated with the latest regulatory requirements and ensure that the family's affairs comply with these laws.

Sensitive information

The offices are entrusted with sensitive personal and financial information from families, and any mishandling or breach of this information can lead to legal complications and loss of trust. Investing in solid security protocols and regular staff training is crucial to avoid such situations. Advisors must ensure that the family's data is secure and protected from cyber threats.

Clear communication is critical to preventing misunderstandings and dissatisfaction among family members. Communicate regularly and transparently, aligning the communication with the client's preferences for clarity and to foster a harmonious relationship. Advisors must proactively communicate with the family and inform them about any changes affecting their financial affairs.

Battles

Conflicts can arise between or within a family. A lack of an apparent conflict resolution mechanism or poor handling of conflicts can escalate issues and damage relationships. Proactive conflict management and resolution are essential. Advisors must be trained in conflict resolution and proactive in managing disputes.

Succession planning is crucial to avoid chaos and conflicts during generational transitions. Early planning and involving the next generation in decision-making can help ensure a smooth transition that aligns with the family's goals and values. Advisors must work closely with the family to develop a succession plan that meets their needs.

Other elements

While cost management is essential, focusing solely on cutting costs can lead to suboptimal service and client dissatisfaction. For long-term success, balancing cost-effectiveness with quality and value is crucial. Advisors must ensure that the family is getting value for their money and that the services provided meet their needs.

Neglecting to invest in technology can hinder efficiency, reporting, and client interaction in an increasingly digital world. Selecting and implementing technology that aligns with the family office's needs and goals for modern and competitive operations is vital. Advisors must keep updated with the latest technology and ensure the family gets the best value from their technology investments.

Narrow minds

Focusing on a narrow set of investment options may not align with the families' risk tolerance and financial goals. Proper diversification, aligned with the family's objectives, is crucial for balanced portfolio management. Advisors must work closely with the family to develop an investment strategy that meets their needs.

Other considerations

For families with strong philanthropic inclinations, paying attention to the alignment between investments and philanthropic goals can lead to satisfaction. Incorporating philanthropic values into strategies can enhance engagement and satisfaction. Advisors need to be aware of the family's charitable goals and work with them to align their investment strategy with those goals.

Assuming that the family office can manage all aspects internally may lead to gaps in expertise. Collaborating with external experts when needed ensures that clients receive specialized knowledge and service. Advisors need to work with external experts when appropriate to provide the best service to the family.

The needs of a family

The needs of families evolve, and so should the services and strategies of family offices. It's essential to continuously improve and seek feedback to ensure consistency and alignment with client needs.

By recognizing and proactively avoiding these traps and errors, family offices can provide a more effective, responsive, and satisfying experience for the families they serve.

Ninety-nine percent of failures
come from people who make excuses.

George Washington

Action steps:

What will you create that becomes and stays intergenerational?

Step 1:

Step 2:

Step 3:

Step 4:

Step 5:

Step 6:

Step 7:

Additional notes and plans:

What are your cost considerations for your family office?
Costs for:

♦ Employees.

♦ Legal and compliance.

- Physical infrastructure.

- IT systems and technology.

- Research.

- Asset management.

- Banking-related services fees.

- External structures.

- External professionals.

- Other.

LDK — LDK

Chapter 5

Managing Assets and Opportunities

From US$20 million to US$X billion

How can one effectively manage assets ranging from US$20 million to US$X billion?

There is always the debate, within the family office environment, between investing directly in assets or through a fund manager.

Brian DeLucia

1 Dynamic and flexible

Family offices are known for their institutional asset allocation approach but tend to be dynamic and flexible. They prioritize alternative investments, such as co-investments, taking minority or majority stakes in businesses, and participating in club deals as part of their overall strategies.

Venture capital investments continue to show upward trends. Regarding sustainable investments, family offices prefer investing in education, climate change, and health, among the top themes.

The critical performance metrics are return on investment, environmental impact, and social return on investment metrics.

Strategic and tactical asset allocation is crucial, and they focus on long-term alignment to navigate potential stress events.

1.1 Capital at risk

It is imperative to comprehend the inherent risks associated with any investment. Each investment carries a unique level of risk, and it is crucial to be aware of these risks. It is pertinent to note that the value of your investments can fluctuate, and it is prudent to consider this while making investment decisions. It is recommended to exercise due diligence and seek advice from qualified professionals before making investment decisions.

1.2 Wider than traditional wealth and asset types

One phenomenon impacting both the creation of new family offices and their investment strategies is the great wealth transfer, which is expected to make Millennials the richest generation in American history.

Alex Murray

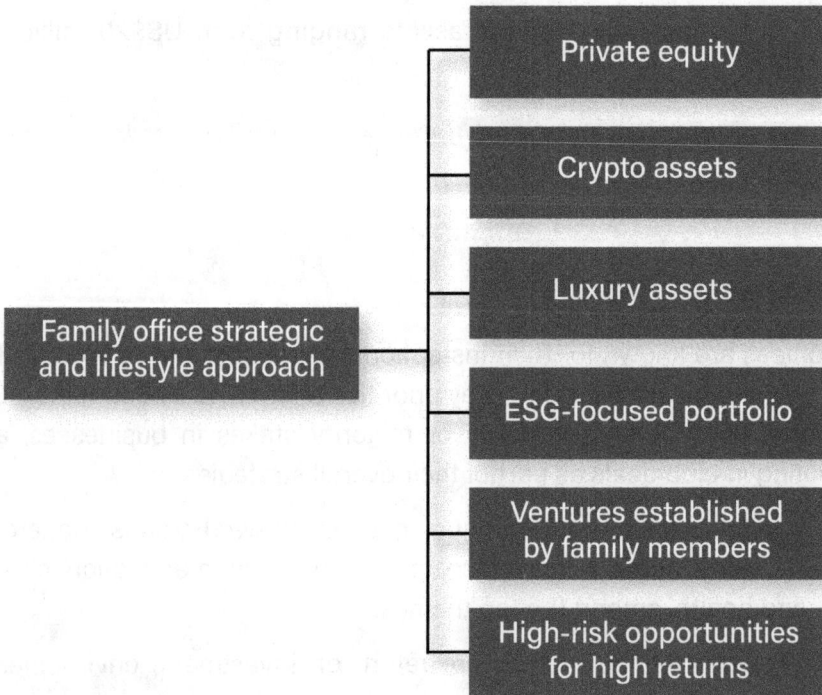

There is a question as to why investing small amounts of money passively in companies is not a viable option for family offices. There are several reasons for this assessment.

It is imperative to scrutinize a company before investing carefully and unquestioningly; supporting a company without proper research and analysis is not an option.

Passive investing has a place in the family office community, however, it gives little control over where one's money is allocated. Alternatively, becoming a partner in a company and having a meaningful stake in its growth and success is a superior option. Otherwise, investing in the S&P 500 might be a more secure choice.

Man is a mental being, and to know this is the first step on the road to freedom and prosperity, for as long as you believe yourself to be primarily physical, a superior kind of animal, you will remain in bondage—in bondage, that is to say, to your own habits of thought, for there is no other bondage.

Emmet Fox

2 The rich vs the wealthy

We should focus on building businesses rather than creating pitch decks.
Brian DeLucia

The terms **wealthy** and **rich** are often used interchangeably to describe individuals with significant financial assets. However, it is essential to recognize that these two groups differ in their approach to wealth and mindset. While both groups are financially successful, the **wealthy** tend to prioritize long-term investments, live below their means, and have a desire to give back to their communities.

Conversely, the **rich** tend to focus more on short-term gains, invest in liabilities, and prioritize their self-interests. It is also worth noting that the wealthy often earn their wealth through passive income streams, while the rich typically earn their wealth through active income from working.

Overall, it is essential to acknowledge and understand these differences to make informed decisions about personal financial goals and priorities.

2.1 Is it true that wealthy people tend to save more money?

Whether households with higher lifetime income save a more significant fraction of their income has been debated for quite some time, particularly when evaluating tax and macroeconomic policies. However, empirical studies have provided valuable insights, revealing a robust positive relationship between saving rates and lifetime income.

Furthermore, while the relationship between the marginal propensity to save and lifetime income is weaker, it still exists and holds importance. By understanding these relationships, families can make informed decisions that promote economic growth and stability.

3 The big picture of family office wealth

An intelligent businessman understands the difference between their emotions and the market.

Brian DeLucia

3.1 The global landscape

The global financial landscape has significantly transformed in the last few years. Unprecedented growth marks this transformation and reshapes wealth management strategies. There has been a shift towards more customized and sophisticated investment solutions. This growth is not merely a numerical increase; it represents a fundamental change in the dynamics of investments, wealth preservation, and legacy planning. Several pivotal factors have influenced this change.

3.2 Rapid growth

The increase in family offices is intricately linked to the rapid accumulation of global wealth, driven by technological advancements, the emergence of new industries, and the expansion of international markets.

Tailor-made strategies that align with individual family goals, values, and legacy aspirations are essential.

3.3 Being exclusive

Family offices provide exclusive control and personalized investment decisions tailored to the specific requirements of ultra-high-net-worth individuals (UHNWIs) and their families. The growing intricacy and diversification of the investment landscape further intensify the need for customized investment strategies. family offices are skilled at maneuvering this complexity, granting access to various asset classes, such as private equity, venture capital, hedge funds, and real estate, thus offering a holistic approach to wealth management.

3.4 Integration

Incorporating advanced technologies has tremendously improved family offices' operational efficiency and analytical capabilities, enabling them to manage intricate portfolios with greater accuracy and insight. Additionally, affluent individuals are increasingly prioritizing the creation of a long-lasting legacy and making a positive social impact through their investments.

Family offices support these objectives by overseeing philanthropic initiatives and sustainable investments that align with the family's overall wealth management aspirations.

3.5 Regulatory changes

Because of regulatory changes, the operation of family offices has become more favorable in various jurisdictions. These changes have brought about benefits such as tax efficiencies and enhanced privacy, making the family office model highly attractive for families seeking to maintain discretion over their financial affairs. Due to privacy concerns, more families are turning to the family office model to ensure their financial affairs remain confidential.

3.6 Competition

The competition between alternative investment firms to attract wealth from family offices has intensified. The fact that these industry giants now recognize family offices as a crucial segment of the investor community highlights the significance of this shift.

3.7 Growth

Family offices are experiencing growth and optimism; however, a few challenges still need to be addressed. These challenges include transparency, infrastructure, and competing with top-tier investment firms.

Despite these challenges, family offices are evolving towards more institutional, efficient, and collaborative operational models. This evolution is leveraging the inherent advantage of patient capital. These models emphasize patient capital, compensation alignment, and family values preservation.

Family offices can use these benchmarks to carve out a dominant position in the investment sphere.

3.8 Global players

Family offices are emerging as significant players in the global financial ecosystem, providing tailored and comprehensive solutions for managing substantial wealth. They offer various services beyond traditional wealth management, including financial planning, tax optimization, philanthropy management, and intergenerational wealth transfer.

By integrating advanced technologies and prioritizing legacy and social impact, family offices are transforming the wealth management landscape, leading a new era in wealth management with even greater sophistication and influence.

3.9 Family members

The younger family office members will be crucial in steering investments towards sustainability. They will be more impacted by climate change and are the primary drivers of the shift towards sustainable investments.

4 Initiative-taking approaches

Initiative-taking approaches assist with minimizing value destruction and protects relationships.

Understanding cash commitment and its representation relative to net worth is crucial. Diversifying into businesses with recurring revenues can enhance your capabilities. Family offices, at different points in their strategic planning, focus on expanding their acquisition strategies in cyclical patterns.

Every individual, family, business, and advisor are unique. Embracing and understanding this individuality helps to establish a strong foundation for a shared vision and agreed-upon value system. Problems can arise when advisors understand the solution and the client doesn't, or vice versa. In such cases, investing more time in explaining the conversation can save resources and time in the long run, or seeking alternative guidance may be necessary.

Dealing with potential issues, such as conflict embedded in the culture, is crucial. It's important to seek necessary care and specialized assistance. Addressing embedded conflict prevents it from becoming part of the legacy.

Understanding the family's goals, their right to choose their associations, work dynamics, and their inner circle brings balance and harmony and minimizes the presence of unreliable stakeholders.

4.1 The *institutionalization* and *modernization* of family wealth

Optimism is the faith that leads to achievement.
Nothing can be done without hope and confidence.

Helen Keller

The **institutionalization** and **modernization** of family wealth are crucial factors in the family office landscape. When participating in the family office world, it's essential to understand the difference between using terminology and comprehending it. This sets you apart and elevates your game.

Family offices extend beyond the traditional sense of wealth management. They oversee various matters, such as involvement with the family enterprise, personal and strategic planning, allocation and reporting on resources, management of family dynamics, and administrative-related matters.

4.2 Investment philosophies

The investment philosophy of a single family office is highly diverse and customized based on that family's specific needs, goals, risk tolerance, and values. Understanding the family's long-term objectives, financial constraints, risk appetite, and values is at the core of an SFO's investment philosophy. It is crucial to consider the family's liquidity needs, time horizon, tax considerations, and unique circumstances that may affect investment decisions.

This includes determining whether the family seeks wealth preservation, growth, philanthropy, or a combination of these objectives. Unlike institutional investors or investment funds, SFOs have the flexibility to adopt a highly customized and personalized investment approach. This can include selecting specific asset classes, investment styles, geographic regions, or industry sectors that align with the family's interests and expertise.

4.3 ESG integration

For many SFOs, integrating ethical, social, and governance (ESG) considerations into the investment process is essential to the philosophy. This might involve avoiding investments in specific industries or sectors or actively seeking opportunities that align with the family's ethical or social values.

Since they manage significant family wealth, SFOs typically focus more on risk management. Risk management can involve diversifying investments, employing hedging strategies, and monitoring market conditions closely. A careful balance between pursuing growth opportunities and mitigating potential losses is necessary.

4.4 Real estate and technology

Some SFOs may have specialized knowledge or expertise in real estate, technology, or a specific industry. Leveraging this expertise in investment decisions can offer unique insights and advantages, leading to a more nuanced investment strategy.

Often, SFOs might collaborate with external investment managers, financial advisors, or other professionals to gain access to specialized knowledge, tools, or investment opportunities. This collaboration should be managed with clear guidelines and oversight to ensure alignment with the family's investment philosophy and objectives.

4.5 The dynamic nature of wealth

Given the dynamic nature of financial markets and the family's needs, an SFO's investment philosophy should be dynamic. Regular reviews and adaptations are needed to align with changing circumstances, market conditions, regulatory changes, or shifts in family dynamics.

An SFO's investment philosophy is complex and multifaceted, reflecting the family's unique characteristics, goals, and values. It requires a thoughtful, personalized strategy that integrates various considerations, from ethical alignment to risk management, specialized expertise, and collaboration with external professionals. It emphasizes flexibility, continual adaptation, and a deep understanding of the family's objectives and constraints.

4.6 Major cities

Major cities worldwide offer direct investment options that attract families. According to the *World's Wealthiest Cities Report 2023*, New York is the wealthiest city in the world, with 340,000 HNWIs as of December 2022.

5 The concept of private wealth management

Remember that the conduct of each depends on the fate of all.

Alexander the Great

For centuries, people have relied on the expertise of stewards to manage and safeguard their wealth. This age-old concept involves entrusting a responsible individual with overseeing one's financial affairs, ensuring that their assets are adequately utilized, and protecting them against potential risks. It is a time-tested approach which has helped individuals and families achieve their financial goals and secure their future.

5.1 Fund managers

One crucial factor when evaluating a fund manager or fundless sponsor is assessing their alignment of interests.

5.2 Sophisticated investors

Sophisticated investors routinely use background checks and other assessment processes to internal and external private security professionals, especially in the post-Madoff era. Background checks on fund managers or new hires are a standard practice that can help avoid fraud and give peace of mind. By requiring a background check, you can weed out swindlers.

While background checks are not foolproof, they can be vital in due diligence procedures.

Investing in a company means evaluating the balance sheet.

To make well-informed investment decisions, it is crucial to thoroughly evaluate the balance sheets of the companies which you are interested in.

Additionally, assessing the leadership team's abilities is essential to determine if they possess the necessary skills to run the company successfully.

Remember that identifying an opportunity is an excellent moment to act and invest in a company. Even if an investor feels it is too early to invest, stating their position is wise and constructive.

This way, investors can remain true to their investment strategy and avoid making hasty decisions that may not align with their investment goals. These investors would rather see more evidence of growth and achieve risk-adjusted returns than gamble on more upside today without enough data.

5.3 Entrepreneurs and asset owners

As individuals who take on the roles of entrepreneurs and asset owners, they commit themselves to the financial industry, actively investing their capital.

This unique perspective enables us to approach situations pragmatically, working together as **aligned partners**. We can make informed decisions in all parties' best interests by viewing situations through this lens.

5.4 Investment themes

Family offices must be able to respond to opportunities and conduct strategic asset allocation reviews and assessments for medium—to long-term portfolio positioning.

6 Wealth management

Wealth management encompasses investment, tax, estate planning, and investment advice. Hiring an **outsourced** CIO is an option that will continue as more family offices are started daily. Existing family offices seek to expand their investing activities and formalize their portfolio management.

6.1 Strategic asset allocation

As sophisticated asset owners, family offices are dedicated to serving specialized wealth goals. A dynamic institutional asset allocation approach, a cornerstone of the strategy, that allows a focus on alternative investments. This includes co-investment opportunities, minority and majority stakes in various businesses, and participation in club deals.

Venture capital investments, a particular area of interest, are carefully considered. Family offices understand the increasing importance of sustainable investments and are generally attracted to investment themes such as education, climate change, and health.

Family offices utilize crucial metrics such as return on investment, environmental impact, and social return on investment to measure these investments' performance.

Strategic and tactical asset allocation and long-term alignment are some of the guiding principles to navigate potential stress events.

6.2 Investment strategies

Family offices' investment strategies are not just a focus point but a testament to our effectiveness. The multi-layered investment strategies, including portfolios with holdings in public entities, cash, fixed income, venture capital, private equity, private credit, direct investments across various entities, and real estate, are designed to deliver results for the family.

The commitment to effective monitoring and control, with execution, is pivotal in ensuring the success of these strategies.

6.3 Public and private equity

Families might make a capital allocation directly into a corporation or project to obtain non-publicly traded equity in the entity. Family offices often purchase a significant percentage of a company through direct investments and expect the equity value to increase over time.

At other times, a family office may act similarly to a private equity investor by acquiring and managing an entire company under the family's portfolio. In these scenarios, the family office will have a skilled team of professionals who are comfortable sourcing deals, evaluating opportunities, and executing complex buyouts.

Investments aimed at non-accredited investors are subject to more stringent regulations. This includes finding new investors and borrowing securities or cash, among other activities.

7 Capital at work

Family offices have significant advantages over institutional investors. They provide more versatility in deal structuring and operations, especially in private equity transactions. Family offices can invest in private markets when the market rallies, while public stock markets remain available.

The younger generation managing old wealth may also pursue opportunities in emerging industries, albeit less aggressively than new wealth. They tend to focus on sectors such as biotech and AI.

7.1 Good fundamentals for infrastructure development

Focusing on practical and achievable goals is essential for developers operating in markets with limited infrastructure rather than speculating and projecting growth. Adopting a realistic approach allows them to identify and address the challenges effectively and gradually build a strong foundation for their projects.

7.2 Patient capital

Family offices have patient capital, allowing projects to develop without the pressure of early liquidation. This also creates continuity and stability during challenging economic times.

7.3 Actively managed investments

Actively managed investment funds are usually a significant part of a single family office's portfolio. Family office investors should still review mutual funds, standard stock-picking funds, or fixed-income managers. However, these investments are already popular among many investors and are more familiar.

8 Approaching family offices

The three-minute rule. This means I am not interested in the transaction if I cannot understand specific facts within three minutes. I believe this rule applies to other family offices.

Brian DeLucia

Experienced investors can be educated about something other than your industry when seeking investment. Focus on providing a compelling reason to invest, like a unique approach, exclusive access, or strong economics.

Avoid wasting time on unnecessary details in your pitch deck and answer the key questions: What's your question? What are you proposing? And how will investors get their capital back?

8.1 Club deals

Club deals are shared among family offices, where they collaborate with other families or private equity firms. There are several reasons why family offices choose club deals, such as reducing risk and sharing rewards in an uncertain environment.

8.2 The real estate sector and other areas of interest

Real estate holds a significant role in the family office environment. It's not just about the family's interests, which can vary from e-commerce to healthcare and biotechnology. Real-world tangible assets, like real estate, are often seen as a more intuitive way of creating wealth than finance.

Given their substantial contribution to global wealth, many families continue to invest in this asset class.

This trend has only grown stronger after the financial crisis, which led to trillions of dollars in investor losses. As a result, investors are now increasingly turning to hard assets for their portfolios.

This confidence in real estate's wealth-creation potential can provide security in your investment decisions.

Due diligence is a critical aspect of real estate investment for family offices. It involves a comprehensive assessment of potential investments, including the individuals involved, the market conditions, and the project's financial viability.

I always recommend evaluating the individuals first,
just as you would analyze a fund manager.

Brian DeLucia

Real estate is a popular investment choice for families seeking direct exposure to assets, particularly multi-family residential properties or multi-tenanted industrial, warehousing, or last-mile assets versus taking a single-tenant risk. If a family has a background in real estate, this can be a natural transition.

However, the process can be more challenging if the family needs more real estate experience. Families should consider a portfolio-building approach, where you have more minor interests spread across numerous assets in diversified geographies.

8.3 Direct transactions

Even when engaging in a direct transaction, you may incur fees if one aligns with a regional operator. If you lack experience in real estate matters, the cost may outweigh the benefits of avoiding fund managers. The operator a family office selects can significantly impact the level of success.

8.4 Due diligence

As part of the due diligence process, it's crucial to thoroughly examine the track record of the operator being considered. Their experience, particularly within the asset class and region the family is interested in, can provide valuable insights.

For instance, if an operator has a strong track record in office assets in the Pacific Northwest Region within the United States and is now venturing into the multi-family residential market in Dallas, Texas, it is essential to proceed cautiously.

Evaluating the operator's performance during previous market downturns is also crucial. This proactive approach can help you differentiate between top-quality operators and those with higher risk profiles.

Quality over quantity

Another due diligence factor is to consider the quality of the team an operator works with and how long they have been working together.

When analyzing a transaction to gauge the team's experience, be cautious if the team has only recently come together and has yet to experience working together on a significant transaction. This increases the uncertainty of working through challenges and other operational inflection points together.

Alignment of interest

After evaluating the individuals involved, it is crucial to determine if their interests align with that of the family. Are they investing enough money in the transaction that is meaningful to them? Are they committed to the debt obligation, or are they asking you to cover their debt repayment guarantees? Based on these factors, one should assess if their financial model is compelling enough for alignment with the family interests.

Additional factors

Additional factors to consider include evaluating the debt leverage utilized to produce returns. We traditionally recommend against investing in assets where the leverage in front of you via debt, mezzanine, and even preferred equity is structured far greater than moderate levels to produce more robust equity returns.

A blend of taxes

Some of the best scenarios blend moderate leverage with compelling tax incentives. However, we caution investors to avoid chasing a substantial tax benefit at the expense of sound fundamentals within any transaction.

Construction and competition

If you are investing in a construction project, what is your competition in the market, and are you partnered with a developer with a strong track record in the subject market?

How many similar assets are you competing with in the market and sub-market where the subject project is located? How many new construction units are in the pipeline and entering the market in the next few years? What is the tenant base in the sub-market, and will it continue to grow? Are there enough quality tenants available in the market to ensure that there will always be a demand for quality tenants if you provide a quality product?

Complex analytics

Performing thorough due diligence is essential before delving into complex analytics. Even basic research requires careful consideration of many factors to ensure accurate results.

Distressed Opportunities

It is becoming more common for Investors to pursue distressed opportunities. It's essential to recognize that intelligent real estate market investors are not interested in partnering with distressed operators. This means that while the asset may not be distressed, the people tied to it are. Instead, they prefer to buy out the borrower entirely and remove the emotional element that often affects poor operational judgment.

If the asset itself is distressed, this is where investors often find compelling economic opportunities. However, while many Investors chase distressed opportunities, pursuing these opportunities you lack, or those you might invest in alongside experience turning around distressed scenarios, needs to be revised. These scenarios often need unique skill sets and temperaments beyond the traditional operations of stabilized assets.

8.5 Second homes and investment properties — considerations

When purchasing properties, it is crucial to consider various factors, including the tax implications for rental income, loss relief, capital gains taxes, and other property taxes. If the second property is held in another country, addressing potentially complex tax issues, and thoroughly examining the structure and funding methods is essential.

Understanding the transaction and associated costs and taxes confidently informs decision-making.

Legal frameworks

Comprehending the legal framework and succession law is fundamental to real estate investment. The ownership structure and purpose of the property are vital considerations. Whether the family or individual plans to hold, rent, or sell the property, various considerations and steps must be taken.

Evaluating the property's financing and the potential impact of currency on any loans is also a critical part of the process.

Property management

It is critical to understand property management, the property holder, and whether the property is classified as a core-family asset. It's vital to confidently consider whether the property is part of the generational story and how the asset will be managed if held directly in someone's will. Engaging with a professional in this field is beneficial and essential for effectively managing a family's real estate portfolio. Various systems are available to help families keep track of their properties. Understanding whether the property is held directly or through a structure is vital to this process.

Distressed borrowers

It's essential to recognize that intelligent real estate market investors are not interested in partnering with distressed borrowers. Instead, they prefer to buy out the borrower completely. This means that while the asset itself may not be distressed, the borrower is. As a result, there needs to be more incentive for the partners to stay in the transaction. It's worth noting that a limited pool of capital Is available for those seeking limited partners to acquire assets, which contrasts with recent history.

Unless you are syndicating investors, finding partners who will invest with you can prove challenging unless you have a compelling story well-aligned with the investor's interests.

9 Private markets

To do direct investing, you have to have
the discipline to do the diligence.

Tony Pritzker

9.1 Alternative investments

Family offices are highly desirable clients for alternative investments. Traditionally, they have been interested in preserving wealth through stocks and bond portfolios. However, nowadays, they are more like institutional investors, seeking higher returns through long-term investments in private equity, venture capital, hedge funds, infrastructure, and real estate.

Unfortunately, the past couple of years have been challenging for these types of investments, with private equity, venture capital, and hedge funds experiencing lower returns.

Private equity and hedge funds

The increasing popularity of private equity and hedge funds has led many to believe that the ultra-wealthy invest only in non-traditional, exclusive products. However, working with affluent families and family offices has shown that they strongly desire to invest in hard assets such as real estate, which have a more tangible value.

Hard assets offer a wide range of investment opportunities for single family offices. The private sector provides families unique investment opportunities, such as private equity, venture capital, and debt markets.

Venture capital

Venture capital is funding given to start-ups or other young businesses that show potential for long-term growth. Private equity and venture capital buy diverse types of companies, invest different amounts of money, and claim different amounts of equity in the companies they invest in.

Private equity (PE)

Capital investment is made into companies that are not publicly traded. Most PE firms are open to accredited investors or those deemed high-net-worth, and successful PE managers can earn millions of dollars a year. Leveraged buyouts (LBOs) and venture capital (VC) investments are key PE investment sub-fields.

Hedge funds

Families may consider establishing a family office when a hedge fund or private equity fund manager redeems out to third-party investors and the fund manager evolves into a family office. The family office serves as a conduit for the principal family members, providing ongoing support and guidance as the family's wealth management needs to evolve.

Co-investment among family offices

Historically, ultra-high-net-worth individuals and family offices have relied on close personal relationships that allow activities to be dealt with discreetly and with a level of trust.

We often hear that family offices are co-investing more frequently. This is not innovative, as ultra-high-net-worth individuals have co-invested together for multiple generations.

However, modern connectivity within family office ecosystems is designing a more structured collaboration. This approach conceptually enables families from different or similar backgrounds to pool their resources, leverage their strengths, and minimize risk.

It is crucial to emphasize the necessity of conducting thorough due diligence in any investment opportunity. This process ensures that interests are aligned, and the operators have robust domain experience, clear exit strategies, and effective governance to tackle potential challenges.

By aligning investments with past domain experiences or comparable scenarios, investors can leverage their strategic value, and skill sets, to navigate potential challenges, leading to better performance.

Governance framework for investments

By implementing a robust **governance framework for investments**, families can achieve their investment objectives and fortify their financial security. Diversifying portfolios and meticulously selecting and monitoring assets are critical steps in this process, providing a safety net against potential market fluctuations.

10 High-risk assets, general asset protection strategies, types of family offices

It is better to live as a lion for one day
rather than one hundred years as a sheep.

African proverb

10.1 High risk assets

Ring-fencing high-risk assets as part of an asset protection strategy is advisable. Advisors should carefully examine each type of asset, analyze the associated risks, consider methods to mitigate them, and evaluate the impact of asset holding structures or the lack thereof. Risk factors and asset protection strategies should be actively reviewed, and their presence should remain a critical item on the family office agenda.

When it comes to family matters, it is essential to seek specialized advice. Relying solely on a generalist may yield less-than-optimal results. Responding appropriately to the family's risk appetite and other issues that impact their overall wealth and sustainability goals and strategies can secure the best outcome for the family.

The approach and oversight of these matters will vary depending on the family's type of family office.

10.2 Top concerns and risks

A spectrum of primary concerns exists in the realm of family offices.

For example, inflation may emerge as the foremost concern among Latin American family offices, which harbor geopolitical apprehensions. Family offices with operational businesses tend to be more preoccupied with technological disruptions than those without.

Family offices commonly bolster portfolio liquidity or diminish exposure to more precarious asset classes when mitigating risk within their portfolios. Risk tolerance often correlates with the generational cohort at the helm of the family office.

In instances where China's inaugural tech entrepreneurs have established prominent family offices, their innovative zeal frequently translates to a relatively assertive investment approach.

Conversely, in families where leadership transitions to the second or third generation, priorities tend to pivot towards legacy preservation and the sustained, long-term growth of wealth, thus fostering a more conservative stance during this generational shift.

10.3 Social capital

A family is like a forest; when you are outside, it is dense,
and when you are inside, you see that each tree has its place.

African proverb

Social capital in this context refers to the network of social relationships, norms, and values facilitating cooperation and coordination among individuals and groups. In the context of families, social capital is a critical factor that enables them to achieve their long-term strategic objectives and uphold their shared values.

Families can leverage their social capital to create a sustainable and resilient family office by fostering relationships with trustworthy individuals who share common interests and goals.

The exchange of information, ideas, and knowledge among like-minded individuals enhances the family's ability to make informed decisions and navigate complex challenges.

Social capital is an essential resource that can help families build stronger, more cohesive, and prosperous communities.

Social capital could also mean the commitment to social justice

This movement recognizes the importance of working closely with social justice leaders, families, and organizations to address the critical issues impacting communities most affected by injustice.

By fostering a collaborative approach, stakeholders aim to create a shared understanding and work towards finding practical solutions to bring about positive change for all.

10.4 Assets that hold an emotional attachment

Although it can be challenging to part with assets that hold sentimental value, it is crucial to acknowledge that there may not be a market for such assets. Wise individuals understand this and take the necessary steps to move forward.

10.5 Impact when families, an individual within the family or business, or assets go global

Family members should be
good stewards of the family and the business story,
taking care of something bigger than yourself and your story.

Anne Klein

Family offices must understand and track the impact on families, their international asset holdings, or businesses when they expand globally, where you must deal with multi-jurisdictional operations and regulations.

Strategy is a crucial component for success; defining the steps to accomplish the goals, be it your professional, business, or personal goals, will set the stage for structured planning and future success.

There are a few essential matters to consider, such as how committed you are to continuing with the business, what role the family will play in the future, what the relationship and management dynamics are, and what the future of your industry is.

♦ What are its competitive advantages or disadvantages?

♦ How will you unpack the opportunities to make your family's future fit and multi-generational?

10.6 Wealth stewards

Being a steward of your family business and wealth story ensures that the wealth can grow in one's capacity as a placeholder rather than a pure consumer of wealth. As businesses grow, the complexities increase, and family businesses should ideally retain their competitive advantage by understanding the inherent goals and dreams that bind them.

Although one cannot choose one's family and cannot always change the team that the family businesses deploy, one could use the dynamics of your shared goals and visions to switch to the next level.

10.7 Manager selection

It is pertinent for fund managers and placement agents to focus their efforts on engaging with family offices. Understanding the substantial variances among funds and their managers is crucial.

It is often asserted that the majority, roughly 90 out of 100 managers, fall within the industry's solid but less impactful segment. These managers exhibit quality in their approach; however, their strategies and performance do not significantly influence the market. Approximately seven to eight managers out of 100 present promising attributes and potential for growth, yet they must still substantiate their ability to oversee a fund effectively.

Finally, within the percentile, one to two managers out of 100 immediately captivate the attention of family offices. These top-tier managers, constituting the upper 2%, demonstrate unwavering confidence in their strategy, possess exclusive insights that set them apart, and exhibit a clear path to delivering compelling financial outcomes. Crucially, such managers have adeptly aligned their fund's structure, mitigating risks and ensuring alignment with the interests of their investors.

The importance of savvy manager selection among family offices includes evaluating managers who previously experienced a down-market cycle. When the market provides tailwinds, excellent returns are easy to produce.

10.8 Fees, costs, and general

The discussion within family offices typically commences with a focus on fees. Observing values and standards is essential for most family offices, particularly if the manager can demonstrate a history of delivering solid returns. This represents a significant divergence. Most family offices tend to engage with inaugural fund managers, even those with a proven track record in their respective domains, before raising funds. Our primary recommendation for inaugural fund managers is establishing a track record through a modest fundraising effort. It is more advantageous to commence with less capital and surpass expectations rather than overestimate the potential fundraising amount. To distinguish oneself from the first fund, offering a unique proposition and minimizing management fees is advisable.

Utilize the initial fund to demonstrate to investors that you can deliver on performance while providing them with a favorable arrangement. Instead of seeking a 20% share, consider aiming for a range between 10% and 15%.

An additional consideration could involve offering a sidecar option, especially for family offices with a stronger inclination toward direct investments.

10.9 Luxury and riskier asset type advisory

The administration associated with owning luxury assets, including yachts, aircraft, art, antique cars, and horses, brings unwelcome complexities. Working with experts who can guide you in the most tax-efficient way to deal with the assets is essential. For example, VAT and other tax issues are involved in operating yachts and aircraft. There are also financial, operational, and reputational risk issues.

Aircraft/Aviation

While selecting and using private aviation might need to be more consistent, seeking expert advice is critical. Specific key considerations are essential when one has "light users" in a category typically called ad hoc or "on-demand" charter usage.

For example, they choose the operator wisely, consider the aircraft's safety records, and understand the contractual arrangements, to name a few. For instance, what are the refund options for trip cancellation when reviewing the guarantees? This ensures you know whether you can list the insured persons on the insurance policy or request a waiver or subrogation.

While the on-demand charter packages have evolved, access and flexibility may differ.

Another option to consider is fractional ownership, while the leasing option remains. Family offices and corporations may wish to avoid asset volatility and upfront capital investments. They might prefer an ownership option. Families typically consist of more than one family unit, and an aviation program will facilitate the lifestyles of the family members.

Consider hiring a professional company to care for the family's aviation needs. Appointing a professional management company has advantages, like bulk discounts on fuel, maintenance, control, and oversight.

Yachting

Family offices often view yachts as assets that demand disproportionate attention. In this context, specialized service providers are well-positioned to assist family offices with this niche asset category, which, despite its value, represents only a tiny aspect of their overall responsibilities.

One of the main reasons family offices face challenges in managing their assets is their limited mobility across different jurisdictions. In many cases, these assets cannot quickly adapt their operations or change their country of registration, making it difficult for family offices to manage them efficiently.

Yacht ownership is a luxury that provides owners with complete privacy while offering a change of scenery. From exploring different countries in the Mediterranean to visiting the Caribbean islands or even venturing to the polar regions, yacht owners can fulfill their wanderlust in style. Some yacht owners may lease their vessels to third parties to offset operational expenses. However, managing such an arrangement's logistical and administrative aspects can take time and effort.

This is where family offices come in, as they specialize in handling these tasks for yacht owners. Family offices are responsible for managing the financial administration of the yacht, providing a significant degree of oversight and control. This includes approving expense invoices, tracking expenses, and ensuring all financial transactions are correctly recorded and accounted for.

Additionally, family offices provide online visibility and reporting integration, making it easy for yacht owners to access and consolidate financial information into a more comprehensive family reporting structure. By entrusting these responsibilities to a family office, yacht owners can focus on enjoying their vessels without worrying about the financial and administrative details.

Music royalties

Some family offices turn towards alternative assets, such as music royalties. Digital streaming could function as a revenue wave. Stephen Hendel and the private equity firm KKR & Co purchased Kobalt Capital's music rights portfolio for US$1.1 billion. According to Reuters, the portfolio had more than 62,000 copyrights at the time of the deal. The long lifespan of songs makes them a steady source of cash flow.

Family offices with the proper knowledge and sophistication typically have an astute understanding of navigating this niche asset class.

Even if challenges are honest and expert knowledge and support are required, before debarking on any investment, it remains essential to understand the specific sector you wish to participate in.

10.10 Luxury items

Artwork, classic cars, and fine wine are often viewed as having investment potential and are collectively referred to as 'alternative investments.'

There can be no fine art without due diligence.

Ty Murphy

Art advisory and collection

In wealth management, family offices are pivotal in managing the financial affairs of high-net-worth individuals and families. These offices consistently seek innovative ways to diversify their investment portfolios and explore alternative asset classes. One such emerging trailblazing trend is the inclusion of blue-chip art collections as part of their investment strategy. However, it's vital to prioritize due diligence before stepping into this exciting new territory.

Blue-chip art always refers to artworks created by renowned and established artists whose works have consistently achieved high market value. The art market has experienced significant growth in recent years, and investors have recognized the potential of art as an alternative investment asset. Blue-chip art offers stability, long-term appreciation potential, and a hedge against economic downturns, making it an attractive choice for family offices. Therefore, investing in blue-chip art is a wise investment strategy that can yield high returns.

Risk appetite

As family offices seek to diversify their investment portfolios, including blue-chip art collections can be a lucrative investment opportunity. However, undertaking such a venture requires rigorous research and analysis. By adopting a thorough approach, family offices can successfully navigate the art market, minimize risks, and unlock the full potential of blue-chip art investments.

Authenticity and provenance

The determination of an artwork's value is heavily reliant on its authenticity. Ascertaining the legitimacy of an artwork entails undertaking thorough research into its provenance, encompassing its historical background, ownership, and documentation. This meticulous investigation identifies potential warning signs, such as stolen or counterfeit pieces, enabling family offices to avoid fraudulent investments.

Artist reputation and market demand

Investing in top-notch art mandates a deep comprehension of an artist's reputation and market demand. Thorough research on an artist's body of work, critical acclaim, museum exhibitions, and auction records is essential to determine their long-term value potential. family offices must focus on artists with established careers and a robust market presence to mitigate the risks associated with emerging artists.

Condition and conservation

It is crucial to comprehensively examine the condition of artwork to ensure its long-term preservation and value—art pieces not adequately conserved and maintained risk losing their aesthetic and financial worth. To make informed decisions about potential acquisitions, family offices must work closely with art conservators and appraisers to conduct assessments. Failure to do so could result in significant financial losses and damage the organization's reputation.

Market trends and expert opinions

Family offices must stay informed about the ever-changing dynamics of the art market. They must closely monitor auction results, attend art fairs and exhibitions, and analyze market trends and artist performances to gain valuable insights. Seeking advice from art specialists, advisors, and reputable galleries is not just an option but a necessity to obtain expert opinions and develop a comprehensive understanding of the art market. Sourcing blue-chip fine art can be challenging but a highly lucrative investment opportunity with the right expertise, resources, and due diligence.

Classic car collection

The 1955 Mercedes-Benz Uhlenhaut Coupé was sold for €135 million, making it the most expensive classic car ever auctioned. It is considered a masterpiece of automotive engineering and design, with only two made. Classic car collections have become a popular form of investment, often focusing on iconic models from manufacturers like Ferrari, Porsche, and Aston Martin. However, investing in classic cars requires meticulous maintenance, proper storage conditions, and attention to security to preserve their value.

Investing in cars has long been a passion for automotive enthusiasts. While many people enjoy classic cars for their timeless beauty and historical significance, others see them as lucrative investment opportunities.

Louis Jooste

New car collections

Investing in car collections has become an increasingly popular alternative to traditional investments like stocks and real estate. Collectors seek out limited-edition models, high-performance vehicles, and unique specifications for their rarity, brand reputation, and innovation. However, it's essential to be aware of the risks involved, such as market fluctuations and changes in consumer preferences.

Collectors should consult with automotive specialists, appraisers, and financial advisors to make informed decisions and conduct thorough research. While car collections offer less predictable returns and lower market liquidity than traditional investments, they can still be valuable to an investment portfolio.

It's essential to recognize the unique risks associated with market volatility and the ongoing expenses related to market trends, authentication, maintenance, and storage. Investing in car collections can be rewarding and enjoyable with the right expertise and careful consideration.

Investing in wine

Investing in wine is a unique alternative to traditional investment options like stocks, bonds, and funds. While most investors focus on conventional investments, investing in wine can provide diversification.

Unlike stocks and bonds, wine investments offer little to no correlation with traditional assets. Investing in collectibles like fine wine can provide returns subject to different market cycles than conventional investments. Wine can even be negatively correlated with the stock market, making it an excellent source of diversification. Wine is its value based on factors that have little relation to the economy's performance, interest rates, corporate earnings, or conventional investor sentiment. Instead, wine's value responds to various factors such as weather patterns, harvest yields, vintage, and consumer trends, all of which intersect with supply and demand.

These factors are unrelated to the stock market, making wine investments an excellent complement to a traditional portfolio. Wine's unique source of diversification might help investors mitigate risk and increase returns.

Investment in whisky

Whisky, often referred to as the 'water of life', has emerged as a compelling alternative investment, mirroring the success of wine.

Consider this: in 1921, a four-decanter lot of Glenfiddich single malt from the 1950s was auctioned for a staggering £830,000 at The Distillers One of One charity event, setting a record for Glenfiddich. More recently, an Asian collector made history by purchasing a 'one of a kind' 1975 cask of Ardbeg single malt Scotch for an astounding £ 16 million, the highest amount ever recorded for whisky at auction. These remarkable instances underscore whisky's potential as a valuable addition to an investment portfolio.

Early stage and technology companies

Ultra-high-net-worth investors exhibit a strategic approach to early-stage and technology endeavors. In the case of very early companies, they are known to make calculated investments, understanding that they may only sometimes yield immediate returns. They then follow up with more substantial investments in the few endeavors demonstrating strong performance following the seed stage.

This approach reflects their keen understanding of the investment landscape and ability to identify promising ventures. At later stages, these investors are more strategic with their dollars and usually like to limit their investments to endeavors where they can bring value and founders with whom they align.

These endeavors are even more appealing when they identify founders who possess that "it" factor and the scalability of the business to positively affect a global population at mass levels.

Venture capital and technology

As venture capital and technology work through the next generation, the family office ecosystem identifies opportunities to build businesses by bringing together talent and technology to solve real societal issues and global challenges or improve the efficiency of everyday tasks.

Some of the best bets are on companies active in defense, artificial intelligence, robotics, and biotech. It is increasingly evident that technology is a powerful catalyst, creating higher margins and efficiencies within traditional sectors that traditional family offices are familiar with, such as manufacturing, distribution, and professional services. This recognition of technology's transformative potential drives the interest in technology investments, as they promise enhanced profitability and operational efficiency.

10.11 Mergers and acquisitions

Family offices must understand the two distinctly different approaches that sell-side advisors use to execute the sale of companies. These are commonly known as bidding and strategic processes.

The bid distribution process focuses on obtaining the best possible price and multiple that is likely to close. They often strategize among the highest, lowest, and middle-of-the-curve bids to achieve this. The highest bid is usually unrealistic and may lead to false expectations, while the weakest bids allow bankers to refine their process to attract more pragmatic buyers.

On the other hand, the strategic process significantly differs and often favors a family office. In this case, the seller directs the advisor towards identifying the best strategic fit and a buyer with shared values rather than just focusing on multiples. A strategic buyer is not seeking to lowball the seller but is willing to pay a fair price for the company. They offer more resources and a better fit post-close for the long game. While the seller is also looking to maximize profits, they are more driven by fit than multiples.

10.12 Cryptocurrency and blockchain

In recent years, family offices have been increasingly discussing cryptocurrency and blockchain. Some are curious and skeptical, while sales tactics are targeting others.

For family offices, it's essential to be cautious and avoid falling victim to fraud. While a few successful cryptocurrency investors have made much money, it takes time and effort to emulate their strategies. It's crucial to look beyond the hype and examine the track record of those endorsing these concepts.

Success in cryptocurrency requires a sophisticated approach. Some people choose a conservative, long-term strategy, while others use quantitative strategies with advanced artificial intelligence to dominate the market. Many risks are involved, so it's essential to be discerning about who you associate with. Individuals who need a credible track record have promoted many unsound schemes, often using sophisticated terminology to create an illusory allure. This should serve as a red flag.

When evaluating these ventures, it's essential to consider both sides of the equation. Assess the fund or investment strategy from a fundamental viewpoint.

Consider if the management team is trustworthy, if their plan is viable and economically feasible, and if their leadership and strategy are scalable.

Family offices should seek out reputable professionals through established networks. Dedicating time within exclusive circles is recommended to gain comprehensive knowledge of various facets of this industry.

Distractions

In today's landscape, various channels emit abundant distractions and unwarranted information, encompassing sales strategies, conferences, and hype. Nevertheless, esteemed ecosystems have sieved through the noise to identify the industry's most adept and competent practitioners. Nonetheless, we advocate prudence in selecting associations.

How blockchain technology evolves the next century

In an era increasingly reliant on technology, it is imperative to investigate its evolution. Blockchain technology is leading this evolution, unveiling the potential of its decentralized solutions. Particularly within the financial industry, there is a burgeoning and compelling decentralized solution for trading digital currencies. This solution substantially enhances accuracy and efficiency in market trading.

Furthermore, blockchain technology can significantly reduce complexity and costs in the movement of goods, potentially revolutionizing the traditional banking experience within the financial system alone. In the foreseeable future, personalized banks facilitated through blockchain technologies on our devices may supplant conventional banks as we currently recognize them. Notably, blockchain technology will furnish banks and corporations with real-time precision, potentially eliminating the necessity for auditing firms to function in the future. Similarly, recent elections have magnified our voting system's antiquated and vulnerable nature. Nevertheless, with blockchain technology, we will eventually cast votes through our devices with 100% accuracy and security.

It is paramount to recognize that blockchain technology is not a mere fad; instead, it is poised to become the new infrastructure of our everyday society, augmenting the efficiency and security of our personal and business lives. Within the family office community, we are privileged to have access to individuals who are authentically shaping a generation.

10.13 Choose your risk items and determine your priorities

In today's interconnected world, family offices are broadening their horizons. They are breaking free from geographical constraints, exploring opportunities across borders, diversifying their investments, and adopting a more global perspective. As a result, it remains critical to determine your associated risks and priorities:

- Geopolitical conflict.

- Inflation.

- Real estate risks.

- Higher interest rates.

- Global recession.

- Supply chain disruptions affecting the operating business and investments.

- Financial market crisis.

- Higher energy costs.

- Technological disruptions affecting the operating business and investments.

- Debt crisis.

- Higher taxes.

- Climate change.

- Deflation.

- Migration and its impact on the operating business.

- Global health crisis.

- Food crisis.

LDK ⟨A⟩ LDK

Chapter 6

The spirit of

Entrepreneurial and Wealthy Families

It's easy to find a thousand soldiers but hard to find a good general.

Chinese proverb

1 Family enterprises

There is a relationship between risk and opportunity.
For family offices, strategic risk-taking is a reality.

Brian DeLucia

Disaster comes from careless talk!

As a family enterprise grows and becomes more complex, families may consider establishing a family office to help manage the associated complexities.

A family office can provide support in diversifying investments and growth opportunities for the family and in managing the various aspects of the family business to ensure its long-term success.

1.1 Stakeholder ecosystem

Many people need to fully understand the role and function of family offices due to their self-interest. Consequently, family offices may need to be more receptive to such people. Consider an alternative approach if your focus is on short-term gains and closing deals.

1.2 Owner strategy

When families create lasting value, they combine their family and business strategies, creating a holistic approach. This could be done in various ways, for example, in a workshop format to design a governance structure. During these discussions, topics like the shared values, mission, vision, owner business model, family and corporate governance, succession planning, training, implementation, and integration should be unpacked. The outcome of these actions will differ; however, this can set the tone for a *Family Charter*.

This will assist the family in understanding the key stakeholders, how family membership is defined, the current business model, and how this will look in the future.

- Will philanthropy play a part in legacy planning?

- How will conflict be dealt with?

- How will a review take place

- How will ownership and management be separated

- What is the approach to remuneration for owners and those actively involved with the business?

When entering a locality, follow the local customs

To ensure a family office's success and security, it is crucial to understand how to integrate it into the larger stakeholder landscape. This requires thorough mapping of the process, and a clear understanding of the impact different stakeholders can have. By doing so, the family office can elevate its position and protect its interests while fostering positive relationships with its stakeholders.

Opportunities

Family offices and their consulting entities receive a plethora of investment opportunities daily. However, not all of them align with their current focus.

Nonetheless, family offices have an extensive network of friends and business associates within the industry and other family offices, which allows them to align interests and make more informed investment decisions. Although family offices may receive unrealistic requests, they tend to be more interested in individuals with sound strategies for executing business in local or regional markets.

Every day, the creation of wealth by businesses
is crucial for the well-being of our society.
Brian DeLucia

All by myself

Some families prefer to avoid partners and instead seek out favorable deals.

What are family offices looking for?

Family offices seek innovative approaches from brokers and entrepreneurs when pitching investment opportunities. They are not interested in seeing the same private equity opportunities circulated within the industry by brokers and investment bankers. This also applies to acquisition strategies, where brokers often promote real estate. These opportunities have been seen many times before. To stand out, family offices desire to meet the best people and come across transactions that are unique and not seen elsewhere. In summary, family offices look for exclusive investment opportunities nobody sees.

1.3 Peer-to-peer support and networking

Family offices allow peer-to-peer discussions, where you can exchange shared experiences and find mentor/mentee prospects.

Power in numbers

Who influences wealth matters because they hold the secret to unlocking a better tomorrow.

With trillions of dollars, one can quickly lose count.

Due to the trillions of dollars hovering over the industry, the magnitude of the wealth, and the imminent generational wealth transfers, family offices, their advisors, fund managers, and investors are impacted and exposed to risk factors but can also find new opportunities.

History can be used to one's advantage

History reflects that family wealth will continue to grow; however, more can be done to stay relevant. With the wealth transition, the primary holders will also be primary givers, which ignites the spark for more significant planning opportunities. How wealth is applied will continue evolving, and global dynamics will impact domestic themes. It remains essential to create a secure network and have a family approach to protect the family legacy by utilizing existing frameworks and making them resilient for the future. All stakeholders must adapt by finding unique solutions while relying on methods and strategies that make certain families and their advisors a force to be reckoned with.

1.4 Reality versus fantasy

Inner-circle relationships mean you must create trust and not simply exchange numbers and information. The question is whether the family office environment should be considered an industry or a community. The answer lies in its historical context, future developments, and expansion plans for a better future. The answer will vary depending on your position within the family office network. It is crucial to prioritize human relationships and ensure personal agendas do not interfere with the dynamics and integrity of this vast field. All interactions should be driven by building relationships for better solutions.

1.5 Deal flow mindset of family offices

*Ultimately, the connections you have
can often make all the difference. I can speak from personal
experience on this matter. Whenever a unique situation arises,
I know who to contact to get things done.
Similarly, thanks to the network we built, many opportunities
have presented themselves to our ecosystem.*

Brian DeLucia

What are family offices looking for?

*You will lose me quickly if you introduce me to your weakest contacts.
If you only send me deals, you cannot close elsewhere;
I know you are not genuine when working to establish trust.*

Brian DeLucia

Many principals and brokers believe that a family office is the ideal choice when looking to raise capital.

However, it's important to note that single family offices typically have specific interests and investment strategies. As a result, they are very selective and focused on their investment approach.

While some families may invest in private equity and hedge fund managers, many prioritize direct investments, with real estate being the most popular choice. In addition to real estate, family offices tend to invest in sectors with which they are familiar, often within the same industry where their wealth was generated.

If a family office decides to invest in an unfamiliar field, it usually prefers to co-invest in other family offices. It trusts and feels more aligned working with other sophisticated families with specific domain expertise areas.

Be courteous to all but intimate with few, and let those few be well-tried before you give them your confidence.

George Washington

2 How private wealth holds the key to economic development and infrastructure

This is how we make things happen.

We bring people, resources, and natural capital together.

2.1 Getting transactions done

*As a family office professional,
it is crucial to prioritize commitment and
cultivate robust relationships,
as these are significant factors in the industry.*

Brian DeLucia

Unfortunately, many professionals in this industry present random transactions and poorly crafted documents that are challenging to decipher.

It is recommended that ***intermediary parties*** attempt to facilitate value that would align their interests with that of the family office and avoid complicating their jobs.

The role of intermediaries

Intermediaries should invest time to understand family offices and avoid wasteful activities. The family office ecosystem is about building strong relationships that benefit all parties, not just closing deals and making short-term profits.

By understanding this, intermediaries can develop long-lasting relationships with family offices and provide value to their clients.

Building culture

It's important to remember that everything ultimately revolves around people and relationships. Moreover, it's about having relationships and getting a return on your time investment. You must identify which relationships benefit you in the long run and which waste time.

And speaking of inner-circle relationships ...

Family offices are part of a global community that includes some of the wealthiest families in the world. These families collectively represent billions of dollars of wealth, accounting for 1% of the total wealth in the United States, Europe, the Middle East, and Asia.

Access to this elite group comes at a cost, but given the kind of wealth involved, the price is well worth it. For instance, a few years ago, a technology company implementing a disruptive strategy aligned itself with one of the most powerful Middle Eastern families, resulting in a compelling strategic relationship with unlimited liquidity.

Ongoing transactional support

Families require ongoing transactional support, and family offices don't always have the resources to manage each transaction or potential risks. As a result, the global wealth regulatory landscape has become more complex.

Generational power for greater impact

No matter how paltry its character,
every generation thinks itself much wiser than
the one immediately preceding it, let alone those more remote.

Arthur Schopenhauer

Rapid forward thinking ...

> *If you no longer go for a gap that exists,*
> *you're no longer a racing driver.*

Ayrton Senna

2.2 Changes are rapid

Family offices face a rapidly changing landscape and must prepare for the future to ensure their continued success. One of the biggest challenges is sustainability, which encompasses a range of issues from strategic asset allocation to interest rate uncertainty.

Indeed, family offices must stay informed and take action to address these concerns.

Geopolitical matters

Moreover, geopolitical uncertainty remains a significant challenge for family offices. Global events can profoundly impact family wealth, making it essential to have a clear plan of action.

Custom and standard family challenges must be addressed to ensure the family's long-term success.

Changing the world for the better

Each family's situation is unique, but common strains include securing the future of dynasty families and understanding how families can contribute to societal success.

3 Family office commerce

> *Replace weapons with jade and silk.*

From the first chapter of the "Huainanzi"

3.1 Stay knowledgeable

Family offices must stay informed about changes in family structures, dynamics, and wealth trends. By doing so, they can adapt to their world's new realities, which can help them stay ahead of the curve.

3.2 Governance adds speed and options

Strong governance structures for both family and business are necessary to move forward quickly and efficiently. Family offices can experience delays or unstructured methods, leading to frustration and lost opportunities, and having different plans to minimize the disruption.

3.3 Stay connected through conversations

However, a single conversation can change the course of the future and prevent such adverse outcomes. Therefore, having a clear action plan and staying informed and engaged with industry trends and changes is crucial. Families are increasingly open to selling their successful businesses, breaking away from traditional views of business retention.

3.4 Family office deal-flow nuggets

Family offices have many opportunities to bring together alignments of interest with their relationships, both as principals and consultants. Since family offices are part of multiple inner circles within the ultra-high-net-worth environment, they tend to share a lot of deal flow, strategies, and mechanics of evaluating opportunities.

Family offices consider a wide range of investment opportunities, including entities that cannot obtain loans from banks, don't prefer working with banks, require mezzanine capital, or are searching for a strategic partnership. When you move in circles that collectively invest significant capital, many individuals come forward to share their investment deals.

Family offices are closed groups that get together, trade thoughts, support various strategies, etc.

Perspectives family offices commonly discuss when reviewing deal-flow:

♦ Who are the General Partners (GP) or Partners?

♦ What is their track record, or what have they accomplished as principals in the past several years?

♦ If there are co-partners, what is the governance between the parties— i.e., How do they make decisions and determine accountability?

How did the deal find us?

How did it reach an intermediary if it did not come directly from the principal? What is the context of their relationship? How do they expect to be compensated? Typically, family offices see their most credible deal flow from a small network of colleagues with whom they have an existing relationship.

How much capital is the GP contributing to the transaction?

What accurate alignment of interest are they bringing to the transaction? Beyond the capital, what are their daily operational capabilities and track record?

Where is the value play?

In real estate, it might be a specific thesis involving deferred maintenance or poor asset management. An established company needs more vital strategic leadership and fresh capital to scale to the next level in manufacturing, logistics, distribution, or product businesses. Family offices always seek to identify pragmatic value creation and avoid strategies created through financial engineering.

What are the returns?

While the track record of the principals and risk factors carry substantial weight during the first conversation — whether it moves beyond the initial level, is determined by the returns or whether the expectations within the financial model are aligned with those of the family office.

Meanwhile, family, friends, and high-net-worth investors are excited to invest in great ideas. ultra-high-worth families look for the alignment of interest and compelling reasons to become a strategic partner or issue a loan.

Here are some other nuggets to consider in the ultra-high-net-worth environment:

Proposals tend to go into an email inbox and out just as quickly if there is no relationship with the recipient.

Brian DeLucia

Expect to hear much of or variation of the word "no" quite often. Family offices say the word "no" a lot. Family offices all generate more revenue by saying "no" a lot. It is a fact of reality.

A typical family office might only make three to four investments per year. Just imagine how often family offices say "no" throughout the year.

Family offices tend to be very discreet and respectful of an opportunity ... unless there are circumstances that warrants a sense of protection.

This means proposals and, most importantly, the people behind those proposals are treated with intense due diligence. It cannot be understated how necessary due diligence is for families.

4 General planning tips for family offices and family enterprises

He that marries for money will earn it.

American proverb

4.1 Be ready for action

Understanding the regulatory framework, tax rules, and their consequences is essential from a risk, reputational, and cost point of view. Maintaining an up-to-date handrail note for the family and various entities outlining the tax treatment and impact will assist in streamlining the decision-making process, reporting, and cash flow analysis.

Seeking specialist advice and support to unpack and comprehend the far-reaching tax and risk considerations is essential, considering the implications on multiple entities and asset classes from local and international perspectives.

4.2 A solid foundation is built on substance

If you want to know what a man's like, take a good look at how he treats his inferiors, not his equals.

Sirius Black to Ron, Harry Potter and the Goblet of Fire

Family-run businesses can significantly impact both the family and the company itself. For a family business to thrive in the long run, family members must establish a solid foundation of shared values. This foundation ensures that the principles, rules, and regulations that govern the business align with the family's values.

Define your board

An effectively organized board is imperative in propelling a family-owned enterprise to the next echelon of success. The composition and framework of the board play a pivotal role in delineating, invigorating, and safeguarding a multi-generational family business and its enduring legacy. Including adept, seasoned professionals with diverse viewpoints, proficiencies, and expertise is fundamental to the assembly of the board. This ensures the board can offer astute counsel and direction to the family enterprise.

Furthermore, the board's framework should foster efficient decision-making and unambiguous communication channels among board members and the family business. This can be achieved by establishing explicit roles and responsibilities, regular meetings, and implementing effective reporting and feedback mechanisms.

Additionally, the board must harmonize the interests of the family and the enterprise while acting in the best interest. This necessitates a deep understanding of family dynamics and business operations and an unwavering commitment to equity and transparency.

Overall, a well-structured board can be a valuable asset to a family enterprise and contribute to its long-term prosperity and resilience.

Strategy defined

Strategic planning plays a vital role in the success of family businesses. It involves defining steps to achieve specific professional, business-related, or personal goals. Establishing a structured planning process is crucial to ensuring future success.

Developing a strategic plan involves considering several key factors. These include the family's commitment to continuing the business, the family's role in the company's future, the dynamics of the management and relationships within the family, the future of the industry, and the competitive advantages or disadvantages.

4.3 The role of non-family-owned businesses

Even an upright official finds it hard to settle a family quarrel. Family businesses are distinct from non-family-owned companies in several ways. The family's values, history, and traditions are significant in decision-making.

Therefore, it is essential to understand and consider these factors when managing a family business.

Keep it real

Effective communication is crucial to avoiding misunderstandings, conflicts, and resentment within the family. Establishing a transparent and open communication channel among all family members and stakeholders is essential. This helps ensure everyone's voices are heard and all ideas and concerns are addressed and considered.

The other night I ate at a real nice family restaurant.
Every table had an argument going.

George Carlin

Successful families access international tax expertise and guidance to navigate complex tax and advisory codes. Families strive with well-crafted stories, a clear strategy, a strong stakeholder network, open communication lines, and a sense of belonging. A formal dispute resolution strategy, captured in the *Family Charter,* empowers future generations, creating a seat at the table while numbers and complexities grow.

Conflict resolution

The importance of people and relationships remains central to the family office culture. However, the way things are perceived is subject to change.

Conflict resolution is another critical aspect of managing a family business. Conflicts are inevitable but can be resolved if family members are willing to work together to find a solution. Establishing a process for resolving disputes that is fair, transparent, and impartial is essential. This helps prevent disagreements from escalating and becoming destructive to the family and the business. Family shame should not be spread abroad.

Maintain and manage family harmony and expectations

Also, governance structures are essential to maintaining family harmony and ensuring business success. They provide a framework for decision-making, accountability, and transparency. They help establish clear roles and responsibilities for family members and ensure the business is run professionally and responsibly.

4.4 Keep the uniqueness of the family

Family enterprises require a unique management approach that considers the family's values, history, and traditions. Effective communication, conflict resolution, and governance structures are essential to maintaining family harmony and ensuring business success. Remember ...

An old warhorse in the stable still longs to gallop a thousand miles.

Project management

It is all about people who fit the culture. Family offices require formal project management and office policies to establish a professional work environment.

The intricacies of family systems

If small holes aren't fixed, then big holes will bring hardship. Understanding the complex dynamics of a family system is vital to creating a harmonious future. This involves analyzing the family's culture and structure to identify the various elements contributing to its well-being. Moreover, it's worth noting that the most successful family enterprises have been philanthropic, even during economic downturns.

Family enterprises must adapt and innovate to survive challenging times, And family offices, as the custodians of family wealth, are ideally positioned to impact philanthropy significantly.

Family offices can have a more profound effect by applying business strategies to philanthropic pursuits. This approach involves unpacking and securing the family's values, interests, and goals.

It's important to note that the content of this book *is not intended as an investment recommendation*. Prospective investors should consult their counsel, accountants, and professional advisors before making investment decisions.

Finally, it's essential to remember that past performance does not guarantee future results.

4.5 Practitioner-based value-creation

When family offices engage in discussions, they often discover much-shared value. Ultra-high net-worth families have trusted friends within the industry to turn to for almost any need. This allows anyone working with them to connect to their relationships and get things done with peace of mind.

Who Gets The Smart Money?

> *If you prioritize your interests only, you will not be able to make much progress in the family office environment.*

Many family offices have a successful record of owning and operating businesses and real estate portfolios. This holds for numerous successful families. Consequently, an increasing number of individuals consistently present their business proposals to family offices, seeking their involvement.

While family offices have access to numerous deal flows, only a few make it to the desks or round-tables of ultra-high-net-worth (UHNW) family investors. Approximately 90% of proposals consist of flashy documents supported by individuals who believe they are the next Mark Zuckerberg but need more substantial backing.

Most of these proposals contain generic information to educate family offices about the industry they are attempting to conquer.

While many professionals float ideas or suddenly believe they could lead a company, family offices prefer to see a track record as a principal operator rather than a project manager, banker, or advisor who suddenly believes they could be a principal.

However, family offices occasionally support a long-time C-Suite executive who is considering going out independently if the economic interests align.

Here are a few key fundamentals we pull from proposals within minutes:

Your money ...

Family offices prefer to see operators with a stake in the game and a reasonable amount of their own money at risk; then, there is a natural alignment of interest. It is easy to walk away when you have nothing to lose.

Intel ...

> *Most pitches tell me something I already know.*
> *Tell me something proprietary where you have an*
> *inside edge to create differentiation.*
> *There are plenty of "me too" opportunities out there.*
>
> Brian DeLucia

Your plan ...

> *Achieving a goal often demands significant effort and*
> *requires collaboration among numerous dedicated individuals.*
>
> Brian DeLucia

Family offices see the same generic value-add strategy in real estate but rarely specific to an asset. In proposals for operating businesses, most principals tell us they will run online advertising, reach a revenue point, and then go for an IPO.

This *is not* a plan.

Profitability ...

> *I will never understand businesses that have been in operation for*
> *a couple of years and are losing money, ask for someone to inject*
> *significant capital, and still need two years to reach profitability.*
> *This is not a business. That is a leadership problem.*
>
> Brian DeLucia

False sense of culture about getting deals done ...

> *This unique culture creates a compelling environment you would want to support.*
>
> Brian DeLucia

Other family offices enjoy working with one another and are often the first call for potential acquisitions or special situations due to the value they bring. Outside the family office world, unlike many families, they give time to intermediaries within the industry.

As a family office, you naturally see many deals. Family offices also see the *shadows* with deals, connecting them to other family offices, lenders, and asset buyers.

Unsolicited transactions ...

Family offices do not appreciate receiving unsolicited transactions. It has been reported that 90% of what they receive are often their least preferred transactions — poorly documented and lacking thorough research. It is essential to respect that family offices are not in the business of raising capital for random opportunities. They do not allocate funds to unvetted ventures, so it is crucial to approach them with the right kind of opportunities.

Unpack if there is alignment with a family office ...

Family office culture means bringing well-aligned people together, attracting compelling deal flow, and focusing on execution.

Where do they spend their time? What is the existing portfolio or proprietary model? How have they perfected their model and created a niche under the economic solution?

Where is the remaining time allocated? ...

> *We each have a responsibility and are committed to approaching it with enthusiasm and a can-do attitude.*
>
> Brian DeLucia

Under-the-radar deal flow ...

The market is flooded with random, brokered, and heavily shopped transactional opportunities. Family offices look for compelling opportunities and might gain access to proprietary information.

Advisors and "Service Providers" ...

Take the time to understand the family's history, background, and goals. What objectives do they have for the future? Present them with a simple risk and returns scorecard to ensure they understand the balance between risk and returns at their current spending levels and investment performance.

For family offices ...

Taking control of your finances is crucial, which means family offices must identify a clear philosophy that guides investment decisions.

Wealth preservation and growth usually go hand in hand, but controlling how your capital is allocated and how aggressively you want to grow your wealth is essential. It's critical to be aware and informed.

Sophisticated family offices allow service providers to sell them products and ideas that don't align with their philosophy. Attending wealth conferences, engaging with other families with similar interests, and learning from their experiences can help you find like-minded families and explore opportunities to work together to manage your wealth.

Ultimately, advisers and families should work together to plan for future generations. Education and wise decision-making are crucial to achieving financial success.

Maximize financial potential ...

Many asset owners need to correct their debt. Most worry about pricing and leverage. Meanwhile, the imaginative play with debt strategically is to leverage assets with stable net cash flows and pay down the debt aggressively.

Value to the local markets ...

As a family office, our past generation generated wealth by creating value in local and regional communities. While the world has become more global today, we must remember the importance of the local market.

The typical make-up of family offices ...

Many family offices operate with a small staff, limiting their capacity to perform tasks beyond their core responsibilities. Family offices typically maintain a lean structure and outsource certain private matters. Most family offices consist of at most ten employees. Determining what to deal with internally and what to outsource is a critical consideration for these entities. It is common for at least one staff member in a family office to be a family member. Additionally, over half of family offices exclusively support the first and second generations.

On average, family offices assist only seven family members by providing income or support services.

5 Family ambitions

Not every family business begins with ambitions of multi-generational longevity, but that's where the most successful land, even though the odds are stacked against them: only one in 10 family businesses makes it past the second generation. The COVID-19 pandemic and the global recession brought home just how much hard work it takes to create a legacy and how important agility is. And the response from family businesses has been impressive.

Peter Englisch, Global Family Business Leader, PwC Germany

According to some estimates, family businesses play a crucial role in the global economy, accounting for more than half of the worldwide GDP and two-thirds of employment.

The top 750 family businesses generate over US$9 trillion in annual revenues and employ more than 30 million people. Family businesses in select sectors, such as beer and cable communications in the United States, own entire industries. In the wake of COVID-19, family businesses' resilience will be critical to the economic recovery. Therefore, these businesses should rewrite (ESG)rather than simply adopting standard ESG practices, which will help them achieve the necessary resilience.

Unfortunately, family businesses do not prioritize ESG-related activities, as diversification and improving digital capabilities remain their top priorities instead of sustainability.

Given family businesses' significant contribution to the global economy, they would be advised to rewrite ESG practices to ensure their survival and success. By doing so, they can secure their legacy and contribute to economic recovery and the world's well-being.

Create a list of the main priorities for a family office:

♦ Support generational transfer of wealth.

♦ Train the next generation.

- Prioritize intergenerational wealth transfer.

- Preserve the values of the family legacy.

- Provide income to the family members.

- Provide personal support to the family members.

- Provide business support to the family members.

- Provide administrative support to the family members.

- Lifestyle support.

- Invest excess cash from the operating business.

- Consolidated balance sheet management and strategies.

- Other.

LDK ⬤ LDK

Chapter 7

Functionalities and Reflections on Family Offices

You are always in the right place at the moment. If you don't like it, change it scientifically by rising in consciousness. This will be permanent.

Emmet Fox

There needs to be more than governance to provide a complete solution.

Families require more than governance to provide a complete solution to generational wealth. Families and their family offices have many important considerations to reflect on. Despite the various moving parts of family dynamics, specific trends remain constant and should be considered. For example, strengthening the leadership of the family office is essential.

What happens when there is a change in dynamics or circumstances within your family and the family office? What about a significant liquidity event? Are we ready for it, and do we have a plan that can be revisited when the time arrives? It is also crucial to consider family governance structures and formalize them. Have we empowered the next generation and captured the story of the previous generation? What are the disagreements, and what are the topics we agree on? How do we communicate as a family, and how do we communicate with the world and our key stakeholders?

Additionally, families should consider having social events outside the family business arena to determine their purpose. What are the growth strategies, and how do they accelerate as a family? These are all critical questions to ask and reflect on when managing a family office.

1 Pre- and post-Covid era for family offices

There is no doubt that the world has experienced a shift pre- and post the Covid era and that it has had an impact on family offices. Impact retention is now more relevant than ever.

Once you carry your water, you'll remember every drop.

African proverb

The COVID-19 pandemic brought people of different generations together, and businesses faced unprecedented challenges, making trust-building crucial for family offices.

The pandemic has brought different generations together to achieve a common objective of securing stability for businesses and families by driving growth and protecting the family legacy.

The fast-paced shift in the business landscape, coupled with numerous challenges, has created complexity. The landscape is still characterized by disruption, uncertainty, and climate change, to name a few.

Building trust among the current generation is crucial while working towards a shared vision for future generations.

1.1 A word of caution

If you are going to do anything, you must expect criticism.
But it's better to be a doer than a critic.
The doer moves; the critic stands still and is passed by.

Bruce Barton

Understanding and recognizing that our differences are not always a barrier to excellence but rather an invitation to excellence is powerful. Working with families requires multiple skills; sometimes, one must remember to return to the basics for a more impactful solution.

Memento Vivere — remember you have to live.

When the time arrives to exit, we leave the world more aligned with our goals, missions, and values, having remembered to live before we die. Although this Latin phrase holds a positive message, the opposite side of the coin is memento mori ("remember that you [have to] die").

Integrating the realities in the family office legacy plan is an excellent reminder that we need to enjoy the good times and plan for the realities of life.

1.2 Holding space

Acquiring specialist insights and wisdom enhances inspired action. The family office environment contains various types of relationships and skills and diverse levels of personality types; holding space for one another and the industry will help explain intergenerational wealth transfer.

Due to industry complexities, listening, observing, and considering various ideas and solutions is crucial for staying focused on strategic goals despite criticism or disagreements. It is being stuck in a loop.

Stay focused on the bigger picture by building micro-pictures.

Anne Klein

The authors believe that staying stuck in a loop, such as constant criticism or reminders of historical mishaps, focusing on unknown disruptions in the marketplace, unrelated political occurrences, general business challenges, or familiar family dynamics, will dilute the impact of a family office and slow your progress. This belief is based on their personal, business, and professional experience.

If the family and the family office has governance structures in place as well as a *Family Charter* dealing with topics like wealth independence, wealth creation, how one forms part of the family, and what happens when one leaves the family, how do you define leaving the family, or what are the requirements for joining a family?

The impact on the overall well-being of all parties is not to the extreme side; it then balances out over time, and when emotions start to settle, people accept the new reality of the family dynamics. The insider's perspective ...

You might go after it every few days,

but the real winners stay with it daily.

Brian DeLucia

In family offices, strategic planning and design play a crucial role in managing the competing priorities of businesses and families alike. Particularly for those with complex investments and structures, a well-thought-out long-term plan that outlines the family's purpose, values, and governance is integral to success.

Furthermore, *yearly business plans* and a 5-10 year *strategic plan* are necessary to address short-term initiatives and long-term opportunities and achieve the family's vision.

An additional critical aspect that family offices must focus on is *risk management*. It is essential to develop a risk management framework that addresses each area of vulnerability in order of importance.

The complexity of multi-asset class portfolios and complex income allocations across multiple tiers of ownership necessitates technology support that generates timely information for decision-making. As such, family offices should rely on experts to design and implement a technology roadmap that enables them to stay informed and on top of all information.

Governance planning is an ongoing process that preserves the family's capital and well-being, engages each generation, and provides a framework for managing their business and other activities now and into the future.

Developing a family office *succession strategy* and plan is a critical governance component, requiring a focus on four dimensions: leadership, ownership, legacy, and value and wealth transition.

Managed services are essential for ultra-high-net-worth individuals and their families. They require a trusted advisor to manage the complexity of their financial situations.

Would your family office have been able to detect individuals such as Bernie Madoff, Sam Bankman-Fried, or Arif Naqvi?

The case of Bankman-Fried effectively illustrates and encapsulates the recurring elements of a deceitful investment scheme. Similar to Madoff and Naqvi, Bankman-Fried leveraged his standing and connections to garner the trust of investors and regulators who should have identified concerning warning signs.

All three significantly contributed to charitable causes, politicians, and political influencers, conceivably creating an incentive for them to overlook probing their activities or, at the very least, to solidify their images as remarkably successful and principled individuals. Regrettably, errors occur within banks, financial institutions, and other family offices.

Hence, one should advocate for family offices to rely on their independent vetting processes.

> *High-net-worth investors often encounter situations requiring*
> *enhanced internal and external controls.*
> *These may include establishing a dedicated security team,*
> *conducting rigorous financial audits,*
> *and seeking-after legal opinions.*
>
> Brian DeLucia

The main lesson is the significance of conducting thorough research, regardless of the fund manager's or asset operator's success and integrity. It serves as a safeguard against any fraudulent schemes. Avoiding a Ponzi scheme is crucial, but a family office can encounter various risks, even within a legitimate investment.

Simultaneously, it is imperative to recognize that fund managers and asset operators may employ strategies that, while not fraudulent in a legal sense, are crafted to further their interests at the unknowing investor's expense.

2 The power of one's social platform

> *Lately, I have been contemplating the significance of having a platform. In today's world, there's much commotion with people debating ideology, discrimination, inequality, and unjust treatment of certain groups. These are genuine issues that real people are facing together in society. Unfortunately, in many cases, people have remained silent for too long, but today, that's no longer the case.*
>
> Brian DeLucia

What does it mean to have a platform?

> *What I am learning from all this white noise is*
> *that there is a difference we can make*
> *if we rise above the noise.*
>
> Brian DeLucia

In these uncertain times, the world needs new and alternative voices, and family offices are stepping up to become that voice. Their contributions are highly valued and recognized for their unique insights and expertise. Through business, leaders are consistently targeted to participate in panel discussions, interviews, and advisory boards. This creates much noise when these activities involve family offices.

Once a family office is in the public eye, it is approached with a wide range of ideas which are not always appropriate. It is important to remember that most family offices tend to invest in favored industries.

Understanding that family offices have influence in targeted and strategic initiatives through social circles, is essential. This includes aligning with partnerships and ventures created around tangible assets, real businesses, natural resources, and genuine relationships.

Sophisticated family offices are known to be keen within social circles to constantly qualify people, rise above the noise, and give the right people a voice.

Additionally, for those building a platform within the family office community, it can be advantageous to communicate a thesis about something real and meaningful, such as *I want to solve a challenge that affects everyday businesses and people.*

3 How to complete transactions with family offices

As previously stated, It is a common misconception that family offices are always eager to invest in any opportunity.

In reality, only 5% of family offices will even consider meeting with capital raisers, and they typically invest in only 2-3% of the transactions they evaluate.

Family offices come in various forms and sizes. Some exclusively invest in liquid assets, while others operate their businesses and avoid investing in external ventures — meanwhile, some family offices partner with talented entrepreneurs, real estate operators, and business founders.

Capital raisers must understand

the backstory of the family office they intend

to approach before presenting an investment opportunity.

3.1 How do you get through the doorway?

Cultivating solid relationships is the key to successful deals. Many family offices only consider transactional opportunities through their trusted networks, which can be formal or informal, through other like-minded people or their formal representatives.

Therefore, it's also essential to establish relationships with people who trust the individuals or entities with whom you want to collaborate. Here is the caveat — respect everyone's time.

Remember this for the person reading your email:
Of the 250 – 300 emails seen daily, how do you
differentiate yourself from the rest of the stack?

Brian DeLucia

As a sell-side advisor, operator, or manager raising capital from a family office, inquire whether a specific memo format is required following a short introduction to determine interest. This gets the quick "no" that everyone respects.

Additional Points

Instead of cold-calling and pitching a transaction, building a good relationship with the person you're trying to connect with is always more effective. Invest the time into a relationship to build familiarity and trust. Remember that sometimes, you only get through the door if you outline a genuine opportunity. It is essential to be clear and upfront about what you're proposing rather than just asking for a phone call to run a scenario by them.

While some family offices can move quickly to close a transaction, it takes time after relationships are built and familiarity evolves. Pitching a family office with a limited time offer, or a sense of an urgent deadline to close a transaction, is never an effective tactic.

Offer aligned returns to family offices

Although people tend to believe they're unique or
the best in their field, many real estate operators,
developers, business owners, and fund managers
share similarities in their returns models.

Brian DeLucia

Family offices often receive over a thousand investment proposals yearly, some exceeding thousands. When a family office invests as a Limited Partner or Co-General Partner, it usually issues only a few checks annually.

Family offices' consensus on most proposals is that returns are too low, the pricing is too expensive, the proposed structure needs to be aligned, or the margin of error needs to be thicker. So, how can you stand out from the crowd and secure a partnership with a family office?

It is straightforward

If you wish to stand out from the competition and attract a family office as a partner, we recommend creating an economically appealing model for the family office.

Your model should offer more attractive economics than the other 98 / 99 percent of proposals the family office will likely review in the upcoming month. This will help you differentiate yourself and position you as a more compelling option for the family office.

The time you enjoy wasting is well-spent.

Bertrand Russell

LDK — LDK

Chapter 8

General Considerations
Tools, Strategies and Realities

The objective measure of our wealth is
how much we'd be worth if we lost all our money.

John Henry Jowett

1 Governance

When creating a family narrative,
stay mindful of the narrative you create.

Anne Klein

Family and relationship patterns, as well as behavioral matters, can significantly impact family enterprises both positively and negatively.

Understanding how family dynamics affect the industry is crucial to using any issues identified to the family's advantage. This knowledge helps mitigate risks and improve family and business relationships.

Some families integrate certain behavioral risks into their Family Charters. However, it is essential to seek assistance and support when families experience these situations and a paragraph in the Family Charter might not have the rehabilitative impact. It is, however, crucial to realize the impact of specific conditions on the family's overall well-being.

1.2 1,2,3 The power of success and unity in consecutive generations

When individuals from **Generation One, Generation Two**, and **Generation Three** come together and share a common vision, they have the potential to unlock something magical. To attain this level of magic, it is essential to return to the basics of shared values, wisdom, and education and establish a clear mission and vision for a better future.

Behavioral risks

It takes on new joiners to cause harmful disruptions, but if they arrive in a well-managed place, they will know where they stand. Behavioral risks can often lead to family breakups, and it is critical to understand communication issues within the family. An unclouded vision of what each family member must do can help mitigate potential risks. If the family works together to establish shared values, it will be easier to create principles, rules, and regulations that everyone can agree on.

Using this approach helps to create a natural flow within the family and avoids complex systems that can confuse. By creating a commitment culture, family members will work together willingly rather than being forced to comply. This approach can help to identify patterns, communicate openly, and reduce misunderstandings. When faced with unexpected challenges, the family can rely on their resilience to help them work together to overcome them.

Family addiction

> *Recovery is about progression, not perfection.*
> Unknown

In the sphere of extreme wealth and luxury, there is a concerning issue that warrants attention — the prevalence of alcohol addiction and substance use among ultra-high-net-worth individuals (UHNWIs).

While society often equates affluence with success and happiness, it is essential to acknowledge that some within this exclusive demographic are contending with a severe struggle involving addiction, usually concealed from public awareness. The demands of preserving wealth, overseeing enterprises, and enduring constant scrutiny can cultivate an environment conducive to seeking solace through alcohol and substance use. The lifestyle of UHNWIs presents unique challenges that can contribute to the development and perpetuation of addiction. The high-pressure nature of business deals, demanding social obligations, and the relentless pursuit of success can lead to heightened stress levels. It is essential to recognize these stressors and consider healthier coping mechanisms rather than resorting to alcohol or substances for temporary relief.

Additionally, extreme wealth can lead to isolation, making it harder for individuals to seek help for addiction. The fear of judgment and the desire to maintain a perfect public image can prevent people from seeking assistance.

Access to private jets, exclusive clubs, and discreet rehabilitation facilities can also enable secretive behavior around addiction, making it difficult to detect and intervene.

Fall seven times, stand up eight.

Japanese proverb

Treatment for alcohol addiction and substance use among UHNWIs demands a tailored and discreet approach. Given the privacy concerns inherent to this demographic, personalized treatment plans are essential. Specialized rehabilitation centers that prioritize confidentiality and exclusivity provide a supportive environment for individuals to address their addiction.

To effectively address addiction in UHNWIs, a comprehensive approach involving medical professionals, therapists, and holistic wellness experts is essential. This approach considers both the physical and psychological aspects of addiction and incorporates family therapy and support to navigate the unique family dynamics often present in ultra-wealthy households.

Access to state-of-the-art therapeutic modalities and aftercare programs is vital for facilitating sustained recovery, ensuring UHNWIs receive thorough treatment while respecting their need for discretion and privacy.

Overcoming barriers to seeking help and fostering open dialogue around mental health is crucial in ensuring successful addiction treatment for this elite demographic.

Breaking the stigma

*Your addiction is not you, but it feels like you
because you've spent so much intimate time together.*

Toni Sorenson

It is crucial to tackle the stigma surrounding addiction within the ultra-wealthy community head-on.

By promoting open and assertive discussions about mental health, stress management, and the importance of seeking professional assistance, we can effectively create an environment where individuals are empowered to seek help and dismantle the barriers of secrecy surrounding this issue.

Other forms of addiction

Addiction comes in many forms, and it's essential to understand the complexities involved. People can find themselves struggling with multiple dependencies, a situation known as cross-addiction.

With the increasing popularity of video games, it's crucial to recognize the potential for addiction and its impact on individuals and their families. Experts are also keeping a close eye on problematic trading behaviors related to cryptocurrency addiction.

Additionally, the gambling landscape has evolved, with a significant rise in online sports betting. Addressing these changes and their impact is vital, as statistics show a notable increase in participation and related issues.

Recognizing these trends is essential in addressing and preventing gambling addiction.

1.3 Family Charter

Live life as if everything is rigged in your favor.

Rumi

Why create a Family Charter?

Without standards, no boundaries are set.

From the works of Mencius and his students

A Family Charter promotes stronger family relationships, aligning with values, and intergenerational wealth transfers beyond traditional wealth.

What is a Family Charter?

Similar documents are referred to as "constitutions" or "protocols" and are often a centerpiece of family agreements and governance for mature family enterprises; the purpose and origin of the constitution can be hugely different from family to family.

Family Governance assists in structuring, educating, and facilitating communication. It aligns families and supports the protection of the legacy—however, not all families do. A Family Charter needs structure and methods to promote its values, long-term vision, and mission.

Practical example

Some of the most prominent generational families and some unknown but intergenerational wealthy families have used Family Charters. One of the multi-generational families in the United States mentioned that they have a specific paragraph in their charter, which was done by several generations before them. It states that although the family wealth is accessible to the family, each family member still has a personal responsibility to contribute something to the family and to pursue taking care of their finances actively.

A Family Charter, also called a *Family Constitution*, governs various aspects of ownership, objectives, family members, and related matters. Many Intergenerational families have used Family Charters to guide their families into the future.

Families with similar values and beliefs will find establishing a formal governance structure easier. By synchronizing their efforts, families can reduce the challenges that can arise. Awareness of the family system and engaging with family members can lead to a coherent outcome.

Understanding the family narrative and the patterns it creates, where each family member holds a piece of the story, can drive the system. This will bring the family together to create a story that everyone commits to, leading to the development of a family charter.

1.4 Consolidated and individual planning for family members and the holding or asset structures

A fool cannot untie the knot tied by a wise man.

African proverb

It is imperative for a comprehensive understanding of the regulatory framework, tax triggers, and consequences to be in place, along with an up-to-date handrail note for the family and the various entities. Seeking specialist advice and support to unpack and comprehend the far-reaching tax and risk considerations that affect everyone, multiple entities, and asset classes from a local and international standpoint is essential.

2 Navigating taxes

Navigating different tax rules can prove challenging, and adding a tax handrail note to the family office pack would not only track decisions but also create awareness of their impact. This, in turn, would guide the various role-players when decisions are at play or implemented, from distributions to sale transactions and purchases.

Each tax element must be examined; for example, inheritance tax has specific considerations, situs taxes must be understood, and holistic estate planning is advisable for the family.

3 Acknowledge generational differences

Always ask yourself: What will happen if I say nothing?

Kamand Kojouri

Each generational family member has a unique focus when it comes to investing. For instance, ESG-compliant funds, socially responsible investment, distressed debt, and technology, such as blockchain, digital assets, NFTs, cryptocurrency, and tokenization. Integrating these generational views and insights is crucial to the survival of a family office.

4 Family office across various locations

Family offices frequently extend operations across multiple geographic locations in an era of increasing global interconnectedness. As the wealth of UHNW families grows, the appeal of international markets, coupled with the imperative to oversee varied investment portfolios, accentuates the strategic need for multi-jurisdictional presence.

Europe stands out as a continent that established secondary operations. Each region introduces distinct cultural norms and business protocols, which can intricately influence communication and workflow.

Due to the substantial variance in legal frameworks and regulatory requisites across regions, family offices' expanding operations must ensure they obtain the correct legal advice. This demands meticulous compliance to circumvent legal entanglements. To surmount cross-border challenges, family offices must execute strategic measures to cultivate seamless operations across all locations. Managing a family office across diverse locations poses distinctive challenges, encompassing the navigation of intricate cultural disparities, legal intricacies, and time zone divergences.

5 Niche expertise and specific industries

Ignorance is a form of environmental pollution.

American proverb

Families seek expertise in their specific niche area with a view to expansion. Due diligence is vital, and identifying quality opportunities within the family office industry while maintaining confidentiality is critical.

Establishing where the family's passion lies and identifying joint venture opportunities, such as real estate opportunities, requires a good network.

6 Economic models

When developing the economic model for future generations, moving away from whether it leans towards the right or the left is essential. Instead, we should focus on creating a **sustainable model of capitalism** that benefits all aspects of society in the long run.

To achieve this, we need to encourage the business community to take on a more significant leadership role, prioritizing the well-being of society as a whole.

7 Social media

Clear social media policies are also crucial, as they can help protect the family's reputation. It is also essential to ensure that everyone involved in the family office Understands what it means to have integrity. This can be achieved by implementing a code of conduct that outlines the family office's values and principles.

8 Key roles and dynamics

The mother hen does not break its eggs.

African proverb

A successful family office must have key staff members who are appointed, compensated, and retained correctly. The CEO is a critical executive who leads and ensures the family's goals are on track. The CIO is responsible for investments and works closely with portfolio managers and analysts. The CFO manages finances, Taxes, reports, and accounting.

Other roles like legal teams, admin support, and executive assistants have specific responsibilities based on the family office's requirements. Roles might be outsourced depending on factors like the asset holding structures, family structure, and unique capabilities needed to expand and maintain the family's wealth.

A cultural fit and essential ingredients must align with the family. Privacy is critical, and background checks are imperative.

9 Successful families and their alignment with institutional knowledge and capital

However far a stream flows, it does not forget its origin.

African proverb

In the highly competitive world of family offices, access to tailored opportunities and services is essential for professionals seeking to collaborate with them.

Given their vast resources and influence, it is imperative to have a comprehensive understanding of their unique needs. Accordingly, working with family offices necessitates creating Bespoke, highly personalized solutions tailored to their specific requirements.

9.1 Not all communication is effective

Effective communication channels are critical in this sphere, as the dynamics of successful families often involve frequent changes in their affiliations. Therefore, confidentiality, transparency, and clarity are essential to professional engagement.

Do great things, be strategically spontaneous, be present, and stay epic.

Intergenerational families are distinguished by their ability to institutionalize their values, knowledge, and governance structures.

Multi-generational families take a structured approach, documenting their values and future vision through various methodologies.

Seeking the guidance of expert advisors is a wise move for anyone seeking to secure the longevity of a family's legacy.

10 Family tools and strategies for success

As you start to walk on the way, the way appears.

Rumi

Each family office should create a custom toolbox. Below are some ideas of what you need to incorporate. In addition to having policies, procedures, and best practices, the tools below will help you stay relevant.

10.1 Clear communication guidelines

A family with a powerful sense of communication and a strategy aligned with their family has a keen sense of belonging. This also assists in protecting the family story and wealth and binds the family as a unit. It creates a protection vehicle for undesirable advisory introductions.

Understand the regulatory framework, tax triggers, and consequences, and have an up-to-date handrail note for the family and the various entities.

It is crucial to properly understand the complex tax and risk implications that affect individuals, entities, and various asset classes locally and internationally. Navigating through the different tax regulations can be challenging, and having a tax handrail note added to the family office pack helps keep track of decisions and creates awareness about the impact of a decision or transaction. This, in turn, can guide various Stakeholders to make better decisions, from distributing funds to buying or selling assets. To achieve this, it is advisable to seek specialist advice and support.

10.2 Tax landscapes and general compliance and reporting

When planning an estate, it is essential to consider all tax elements, including inheritance tax, situs taxes, and holistic tax planning for the family, as well as each asset class and holding structure. Make sure you have a good understanding of the reporting and compliance requirements.

Domicile versus residency

A dragon's pool and a tiger's den.

From a tax perspective, these two words can significantly impact your taxes. Under common law, an individual can only be domiciled in one place. Understanding how this affects you, one can see that your domicile will remain static.

It is essential to speak to your tax advisor to understand how these terms affect you, your family, and your business regarding the taxation of your assets during and after your life.

Asset distribution and acquisition strategy

Discussions with family offices are typically more "sophisticated" than those with friends and family investors or High-Net-Worth investors. People often mistake confident investors for family offices.

Brian DeLucia

Effective planning involves having an asset distribution strategy and understanding how and where assets are held. It is also essential to seek advice when acquiring assets or a business interest.

10.3 The art of alignment

Have governance structures that *align* with the family, vision, mission, and values. The governance structures can be accomplished through a variety of strategies and structures. The concept of *family governance structures* and *charters* has been an ongoing topic of discussion for successful families. These documents, also known as *constitutions* or *protocols*, often serve as a focal point for family agreements and governance within well-established family enterprises and offices.

The purpose and origin of family governance can vary significantly between families. However, the potential benefits are numerous. Family governance can educate and facilitate communication, guiding the family toward a future based on agreed-upon values, mission, and vision statements, inspiring a shared sense of purpose and direction.

Partnerships

Have a focused approach to partnerships or stakeholder management. This will assist the family office during good times and crises.

Have more than one plan, be versatile, and diversify

It is essential to have optional plans and backup support. Versatility and diversification will ensure longevity.

Mentorship

Every step makes a footprint. A robust mentorship approach will support the family story and keep the enterprising spirit alive. Reversed mentorship serves the family well by bringing in new and collaborative ideas.

Education through a family and business academy

Creating a family and business academy will support the notion of a family that strives for excellence and encourages a spirit of curiosity and learning.

Creativity and a family vision board

Creativity creates better collaboration. This could be done in several ways. For example, each family member can create a vision board. The family can then make one for their family as a collective unit, fostering a sense of belonging and shared vision.

Family enterprises and a well-constructed board

A well-designed and composed board is essential for taking your family business to the next level. This can help shape, ignite, and safeguard your business and family legacy story for future generations. Strategic planning is crucial for the success of your family business.

Shared traditions

Capturing and creating family traditions can enhance the family's story by capturing.

Family portraits

Creating portraits of the family gives a sense of unity and identity.

Family tagline

A family that can create a short and memorable phrase representing them and their values makes it easier for insiders and outsiders to understand the family identity.

Family crest, family motto

Understanding one's history can help families learn valuable information. The family crest is divided into several parts; the colors and symbols hold some answers to the family story.

Taking the advisors on the journey

The stronger the advisory team, the better the chances of survival. The advisory teams must understand the family vision and have strong ethics. Advisory Councils and the selection of the councils help the family go from strength to strength.

Tracking and showing-up

The success of the family office will depend on how one monitors and tracks your success stories. Showing-up and having clear guidelines will guide the family office professionals to reach an impactful outcome.

Physical and mental well-being of the family

There has been an increased desire to assist and protect the family when medical care is required. An initiative-taking approach serves the family better when it relates to health matters.

Integration and unity consciousness

The greatness of the man's power

is the measure of his surrender.

William Booth

Integrating the various practices and shared values will serve as a legacy, determining the goal of staying intergenerational. Integration requires living your legacy, letting go of specific ideas, and enjoying family dynamics and history. If one has done the most with what one has have and what one has, one can more easily surrender, knowing that all is well.

Shifting into different generations

Although baby boomers, born between 1946 and 1964, own the highest percentage of assets of all generations, significantly more than the silent generation before them (born before 1946), generation X, born 1965 -1980, and millennials, born after 1980, also hold a significant amount of power within their assets to bring positive change in the world by using their wealth purposefully. All succeeding generations will have specific qualities and challenges.

Each shift requires integration

Integrating and understanding the differences and dynamics will create a stronger bond between the family members. There are multiple strategies that the family can use for this, such as making a junior governance board, participating in philanthropy projects, and learning more about the family business, to name a few.

Integrating Generation Z is critical, and harnessing their viewpoints can help families succeed in challenging situations. Generation Z, often shortened to Gen Z, is known as Zoomers. Generation Z, having grown up with access to digital technology from a young age, is usually referred to as "digital natives," even if not necessarily digitally literate.

Unique Family members' perspectives can uplift cultures, and incorporating distinct aspects can improve the experiences for a greater purpose.

Interactions

Open and honest communication between parents and children is essential. Without it, unresolved issues will always remain and create tension; if both parties are truthful, love for a more significant cause will eventually overcome obstacles.

11 The psychology of wealth and impact on families

*An aging population means more family offices are
transferred to the next generation —
and this demographic shift is happening worldwide.
With this demographic change comes
a shift in focus for family offices,
from wealth creation to wealth retention.*

Alex Murray

Success is often linked with financial prosperity. Children of wealthy parents may find it challenging to develop motivation, trust, and a sense of agency. Parents must have a healthy relationship with money to provide a positive financial education. Establishing a responsible family culture and a clear direction for the family's wealth is essential.

Studies suggest that children who grow up in safe and privileged environments may develop a sense of entitlement and uniqueness.

Children exposed to sudden wealth may struggle with anxiety, depression, and an altered sense of self-worth. To ensure that children become successful inheritors of wealth, they must be educated in finance and money management and be free to evolve their identity and self-perception.

Defining core values and establishing a family mission statement can provide a clear framework for educating children about family wealth.

Converting principles into actions can cultivate a sense of responsibility towards the wider world and an awareness that wealth can be used for doing good, not just for material gain.

11.1 Sale of a business

Family-owned businesses play a crucial role in our society and communities. They are essential for job creation, wealth generation, stability, and continuity. By upholding family values and traditions, these businesses enrich the social fabric of communities, fostering strength and cohesion. Supporting family-owned businesses is beneficial not only for the economy but also for the overall enrichment of our society.

Entrepreneurs often dedicate years of hard work, take risks, and invest personally in their businesses. When it comes time to sell, it can be a complex process. Understanding the different exit strategies is crucial, no matter when the entrepreneur plans to leave.

Preparation is key

Being well-prepared is critical to confidently transitioning out of the business and achieving success. To make a business appealing to potential buyers, it's essential to approach the process strategically. This involves positioning the company strategically and ensuring operational readiness to attract the right buyers, ultimately increasing the likelihood of a successful sale and achieving the desired outcome.

Risk-assessment

Conducting a thorough risk assessment is crucial for identifying potential obstacles that may devalue your business. Addressing these challenges in advance can improve your business's appeal. It's essential to comprehensively evaluate legal, financial, and reputational risks and develop a strategy to minimize their impact. Proactively managing these risks increases your business's value and helps it remain competitive in a dynamic market landscape.

It is essential to recognize that two buyer profiles target family-owned businesses

The most common are financial buyers, such as private equity funds, who prioritize return on investment when considering investment opportunities. They assess businesses based on their potential for growth and profitability to identify those that can deliver solid returns and offer a profitable exit strategy with an average of *three to five* years.

On the other hand, strategic buyers focus on acquisitions driven by the desire of buyers to integrate complementary products, services, or customer bases into their existing operations, thereby generating synergies and long-term shareholder value.

Strategic buyers conduct a thorough evaluation process to identify potential acquisitions that can be seamlessly integrated, bolstering their competitive edge and creating value for their shareholders. It's essential to understand the motivations and objectives of strategic buyers to inform your preparation and marketing strategy, as this can potentially influence the terms and price of the sale. When considering the sale of a family business, the presence of a proficient management team is crucial for facilitating a successful transition. This team enhances the company's value by demonstrating operational autonomy from the owner, thereby enabling the potential for a management buyout (MBO) with external funding.

Primary options

Owners of family businesses have two primary options when selling company shares or assets. Each method carries distinct implications for both the seller and the buyer. The first method involves the purchase of shares. In this approach, the buyer acquires the business's entire share capital, effectively taking over the company and all its liabilities, including tax and contractual obligations.

This method requires thorough due diligence on the buyer's part to scrutinize the business's legal, tax, and financial standing, often resulting in a more detailed sale and purchase agreement with extensive warranties.

Specialist support

Selecting lawyers with specialized knowledge and expertise in mergers and acquisitions transactions within the specific business sector is crucial. These lawyers provide legal guidance throughout the sale process, ensuring all legal requirements are met.

Additionally, the involvement of accountants skilled in financial analysis is essential for understanding the tax implications of the sale, enabling informed decision-making.

Investment bankers

The other critical professional hire is an investment banker with specific experience with similar companies. They offer a more comprehensive service by developing a narrative that attracts institutional buyers or sophisticated investor groups. Their involvement is more intensive, often reflected in their fee structures, which may include a monthly retainer and a success fee.

Tax matters!

Tax problems can be a significant concern during due diligence and impact a business sale's negotiation and final terms. Some common tax-related issues can arise, and working with a tax expert is essential.

The general take on the sale of a family-owned business

Overall, selling a family-owned business is a complex and critical undertaking that demands meticulous planning and execution. It encompasses essential stages such as engaging potential buyers, handling offers and negotiations, conducting due diligence, finalizing the sale, and transitioning the business.

Each phase of the transaction necessitates meticulous attention to detail and strategic decision-making.

11.2 Critical considerations for cross-border situations

It is common for many large family offices to have cross-border business interests. This means critical areas for the international tax framework must be addressed.

The successful operation of the international enterprise network depends on prioritizing tax compliance, strategies, and adherence to regulations. These elements are crucial in achieving success and sustainability within the global business environment.

Key areas that require careful consideration include:

◆ Base Erosion and Profit Shifting (BEPS).

◆ Tax treaties: Bilateral agreements between countries that determine the tax treatment of cross-border income and provide mechanisms to avoid double taxation.

◆ Transfer pricing is the pricing of goods, services, and intangible assets transferred within multinational company divisions.

◆ Permanent establishment: The threshold used in international tax law to determine if a business has a taxable presence in a particular jurisdiction.

◆ Thin capitalization rules: Regulations aimed at preventing multinational companies from excessively loading their subsidiaries with debt to minimize taxes.

- Tax Havens and Anti-avoidance: Measures to counteract multinational enterprises' use of tax havens and aggressive tax planning.

- Country-by-country reporting: Multinational enterprises must report income, taxes paid, and specific indicators of economic activity on a country-by-country basis.

- Controlled Foreign Company (CFC) Rules: Regulations that aim to tax passive income earned by controlled foreign subsidiaries of a company in low-tax jurisdictions.

- Tax residence rules: Criteria to determine an entity's tax residency status in a particular jurisdiction.

- Tax credits and exemptions: Mechanisms used to reduce the tax liability of multinational enterprises, including foreign tax credits and exemptions for certain types of income.

Prioritizing and effectively managing these areas is essential for international enterprises to navigate the complex landscape of global taxation and compliance.

Economic citizenship and residency for families

Investor citizenship, also known as citizenship by investment, enables individuals to obtain citizenship or residency in a foreign country through making business investments or contributions to the state.

Families are drawn to economic citizenship or residency due to various benefits, such as visa-free travel and the prospect of obtaining a passport from a politically stable nation.

Families must seek personalized immigration advice, including tax and wealth structuring guidance, tailored to their needs. Changing citizenship could be ill-advised without professional guidance.

What measures should a family implement to plan for the future?

Here are some basic ideas:

⇒ *Family governance structuring and planning.*

⇒ *Family retreats.*

⇒ *Business succession planning.*

⇒ *Family council employment policy.*

⟹ *NextGen committee.*

⟹ *Family constitution.*

⟹ *Exit strategy.*

What types of items do successful families tend to collect?

The administration and protection of these types of collectibles require a different approach and strategy.

⟹ *Art.*

⟹ *Jewelry.*

⟹ *Automobiles.*

⟹ *Silverware.*

⟹ *Household items (antiques).*

⟹ *Wine or spirits.*

⟹ *Couture items.*

———————LDK—🌀—LDK———————

Chapter 9

Leadership within the Family and Marketplace

Each family office differs; some specialize in real estate, while others focus on manufacturing, energy, or services businesses. Over the past couple of years, the marketplace needs a different type of leadership to get things done. We have experienced this firsthand.

Why is this?

Trust certainly is at the top of the list. The relationship matters.

At the same time, we also have a different perspective. family offices do not approach things with a mindset of chasing dollars or throwing things against the wall.

From this perspective, we are becoming more valuable in the marketplace. family offices throughout different industries create better places to live and work, more jobs, better economics, and address quality-of-life challenges.

Family offices are seeking to align with talented individuals who could be creating more impact if they had the liquidity support, strategic value and leadership that the family brings to the table. The family office community is beginning to give exciting people a voice and is creating solutions that realize measurable social and economic impacts on communities.

Public and private partnerships

On a much larger scale, powerful global families are bridging the gap within public-private partnerships through real estate and infrastructure to spur economic development and grow communities.

While the priority will always remain downside protection and finding opportunities to generate compelling yields — what creates passion and purpose throughout the day is influencing leadership in communities worldwide.

1 Leadership and actions for a better world

Whoever thought the word *hello* was so powerful?

A long time ago, I was exposed to the power of hello through an old patriarch. He was a real estate developer and was on the road driving throughout most of his days. On his everyday travels, if he saw someone working outside, he would pull over, get out of his car, and say hello! The question would often follow this up: what are you doing? It was terrific the opportunities he would uncover from this simple conversation.

I apply this to my everyday business. Whether at a function, waiting for an appointment, or even on LinkedIn, I often say hello and let nature take its course. By being authentic in my dialogue, I have built many friendships, opportunities, and business alliances.

Brian DeLucia

The conveniences of modern technology ...

I frequently speak with members of our ecosystems virtually every day. It's best to connect and discuss initiatives when you can't meet in person.

It's amazing how rapport develops when people communicate. I also engage in this practice with other colleagues. When you engage in conversation, new opportunities arise. It's a skill that has been lost and needs to be rediscovered. The only way to become comfortable with it, is to practice it.

Brian DeLucia

1.1 The bottom line is to pick up the phone

Building relationships and gaining respect is crucial in business, but unfortunately, many people rely too heavily on technology and need to remember the basics. While text messages, social media, and other digital communication methods are convenient for quick messages and questions, they must include the importance of picking up the phone or having an in-person conversation. A phone call or in-person conversation is often the best solution when discussing complex topics like strategies, projects, feedback, or exchanging ideas.

These conversations foster trust and understanding that is difficult to achieve through text messages alone. Misinterpretations, lost ideas, and misunderstandings can quickly occur through messaging but can be avoided through honest conversation. Therefore, avoiding making excuses and using the phone or in-person conversation when necessary is essential. It can lead to higher productivity and more effective communication. Each situation demands a different level of leadership.

Do not walk ahead of people …

walk with them and be a source of encouragement.

Brian DeLucia

Conventional opinion is the ruin of our souls.

Rumi

Empathetic listening and understanding diverse perspectives
are hallmarks of effective leadership.

Brian DeLucia

In moments of crisis, the wise build bridges,
and the foolish build dams.

African proverb

1.1 Succession planning for family businesses

How succession is overseen within a family business can vary depending on the generation. Social and economic landscapes shift as time passes, and cultural norms evolve. The succeeding generations tend to have different experiences, education, and perspectives. They may travel more extensively and be more comfortable operating in a global technological world and thus have unique ways of doing things.

The second generation is closer to how wealth was created and nurtured within the family. That is why ongoing education and knowledge sharing are vital to protecting the wealthy legacy.

1.2 Running a successful family enterprise

Essential aspects of running a successful family enterprise are clear values, transferring knowledge to others, maintaining the right mindset and founding principles, managing risks, identifying opportunities, guiding principles, and ensuring business perpetuation.

Family governance is crucial to ensuring long-term success and stability for families. However, it only sometimes helps individuals grow and develop.

It's more than meets the eye

In the past, many families believed that preserving and growing their wealth was the primary factor in achieving generational success.

This mentality still prevails among some families today, but many sophisticated families have realized that success requires more than money.

As a result, an increasing number of families are turning towards family governance to secure success across generations.

While family dynamics can be complex and multifaceted, specific trends persist and are worth considering. Families' most common mistake is trying to influence and force decisions upon their children, which often creates long-term conflict. Families must know their children's talents, interests, and personalities. Through self-discovery, families can support their children in identifying their strengths and opportunities to align them with value in the real world. This is where families can leverage their resources and networks to position their children to succeed. However, these activities must align with teaching the next generation a strong work ethic no matter their path.

The following are essential questions to consider for strengthening leadership within a family office:

♦ How can changes in family circumstances and dynamics be addressed effectively?

♦ What is the best approach when dealing with a significant liquidity event? Is there a plan in place that is ready to be put into action and can be revised as needed?

♦ Have family governance structures been established and formalized to clarify roles, decision-making processes, and responsibilities?

♦ Has the next generation been empowered, and has the history and values of the prior generation been documented?

♦ Is there a family council in place?

♦ What is the appropriate balance between family and non-family members on the board, and how are these roles filled? What are the benefits of having non-family members on the board, and will this strategy secure the family legacy and values?

♦ Are regular family meetings held to discuss business matters and address concerns?

♦ What are family traditions, and how do you carry them forward to enhance the story for the next generation?

♦ What are the areas of agreement and disagreement within the family?

♦ How can communication with the family, the world, and critical stakeholders be optimized?

♦ Have philanthropic goals and structures been formalized?

♦ How can social events beyond the family business be planned, and what are the objectives of these events?

♦ What are growth strategies, and how can the family accelerate its progress?

♦ What is the optimal ownership structure for each entity or asset holding?

♦ What education curriculum will be designed for the family, specifically for the next generation?

2 Collective intentionality

The universe is run strictly on the lines of a cafeteria. Unless you claim mentally — what you want, you may sit and wait forever.
Emmet Fox

2.1 Aligning thoughts and actions co-creates a future that reflects family values

Choices we make can shape a new world. Integrate transformative approaches, principles of interconnectedness, and mindful cooperation within the family and family office environments. It is currently a pivotal moment, where a relationship with the Self, the universe, and others need to be created.

Individual qualities bring us strength

We must believe in equal treatment and high expectations for everyone, regardless of background. However, we can also develop practical and intelligent platforms to provide opportunities to those willing to work hard.

Each of us has something unique to offer, and it is essential to embrace the values of respect and leadership to bring positive changes to our businesses, communities, and families. This will serve as a foundation for restoring humanity to its original intent.

Celebrate differences, which foster a world where differences are bridges rather than barriers to cooperation.

The flow of opportunities

You are not meant for crawling, so don't. You have wings.
Learn to use them and fly.

Rumi

It is easier to build strong children than to repair broken men.

Frederick Douglass

If you are a young professional in this industry ...
bring value by working with leadership.

Brian DeLucia

2.2 Essential tools and knowledge-sharing by family leaders

Leadership should be comfortable with sharing knowledge. This would include practical aspects such as managing and safeguarding accounting knowledge, intergenerational knowledge transfer, balance sheet optimization, deal structuring, and financial optimization as they are crucial topics for families and advisors.

Understanding and managing businesses, corporate structures, family governance structures, legal entities, and financial services is vital. Seeking business advice is critical for family-owned companies.

Know your client; maybe they used to know accounting

What if Mick Jagger pursued finance and accounting instead of music? Aspiring family accountants and advisors bring unique perspectives that add value and support new approaches. Let's keep up the excellent track records.

Missing pieces ... questions for reflection:

♦ What advice is needed to take the family and business to the next level?

♦ What are the current trends and offerings?

♦ How do you select an advisory team?

♦ How do you select the right services and products?

♦ What are the industry challenges and opportunities?

Other strategies to embark on.

> *Maybe That's What Batman Is About. Not Winning.*
> *But Failing, And Getting Back Up.*
> *Knowing He'll Fail, Fail A Thousand Times,*
> *But Still Won't Give Up.*
> Batman, Comics (Zero Year)

3 Personal and professional development ideas for young leaders in the family office environment

Be understated and likable and
watch how things naturally begin to happen!

3.1 Building a culture of strength

The bottom line: Hire people who bring something different to your organization. As a leader, I take it upon myself to create a culture of openness to discussing the most effective and efficient ways to make things happen and solve problems.

Brian DeLucia

3.2 Attracting and building a team

Attracting and building a team around the best talent is crucial to maximize any organization's success. As a leader, it is essential to prioritize building a team of individuals with skill, passion, and purpose, as this will make a difference in the marketplace. To achieve this, organizations must create a culture that promotes inclusion and diversity without compromising on identifying the best people. As a leader, you set the tempo and culture of your organization.

Diversity must be ingrained in the DNA of your organization from the very start at all levels, with the inclusion of programs that educate and raise awareness of diversity.

Respect, teamwork, and accountability

This means we must promote respect, teamwork, and accountability through our actions as leaders. Leaders should aim to build teams that bring together individuals from diverse backgrounds who excel in their work and provide them with purposeful opportunities to elevate their brand.

Companies become complacent when they hire people from the same backgrounds, same schools, and for restrictive roles. Your best people will thrive when there is purpose and the ability to work across various units within your organization to make things happen or solve problems.

Go the extra mile and have patience with yourself

You set yourself apart from most people when you go the extra mile. Your most valuable asset is your human capital. Regardless of their background, everyone has something to contribute to.

Find effective ways to encourage people to speak up and share their ideas. Everyone deserves to feel respected in this way. Allowing everyone to contribute leads to better decision-making and results when the team comes together.

4 Legacies

4.1 Ancestral legacies

In family philanthropy, legacy often overshadows succession planning, leaving the organization's future uncertain. Succession planning for family foundations is crucial For the continuity, relevance, and integrity of the foundation's mission, families need to think about who will take over their philanthropic efforts after they have passed away. This is known to ensure that the decision-making responsibility is transferred smoothly. The wish to shape the future of a family foundation is natural. Through succession planning, founders can ensure that future generations uphold their strategic vision, values, and philanthropic goals.

This planning process enables founders to instill a sense of purpose and direction that can guide the foundation, even in their absence. It also provides the flexibility to adapt to future challenges and opportunities.

4.2 Dynamic legacies

The goal is establishing a solid foundation for a lasting and dynamic legacy. Conflicts within family-run foundations can pose significant challenges to their functioning. Without proper guidance and planning, misunderstandings and disputes over the foundation's direction led to deep-seated family rifts. To avoid such circumstances, it's essential to have family foundation succession planning, which serves as a preventive measure by clarifying the founder's intentions and establishing a structured decision-making and leadership transition process. This clarity and structure can be instrumental in preserving family unity and ensuring that the foundation's mission advances without becoming a source of contention.

Societal changes

The philanthropic sector constantly responds to societal changes, technological advancements, and global priorities. Planning for family succession is essential to ensure that foundations remain relevant and effective in this ever-evolving landscape.

By implementing mechanisms for continuous education and engagement of future generations, foundations can stay ahead of the game regarding philanthropic innovation and impact.

It's more than a plan

Succession planning is more than just selecting people to take over leadership roles; it's about getting them ready to lead. This readiness requires mentoring upcoming leaders about the subtleties of philanthropic strategy, governance, and community involvement. Families can guarantee a smooth handover and the continued prosperity of their charitable endeavors by investing in developing their abilities and knowledge.

Family foundation succession planning is not just a strategic necessity but an absolute necessity for founders caring about their philanthropic mission and families. By addressing critical reasons for succession planning, family foundations can ensure that their legacy of impact and philanthropy not only endures but flourishes, benefiting countless generations. Let's not shy away from the inevitability of change. Instead, let's take charge and create a comprehensive plan that secures our philanthropic endeavors and family harmony for the future.

4.3 Women in family enterprises, the gender pledge

Typically, family enterprises possess a distinctive commitment to ongoing improvement and a desire to learn that stems from their founders.

This characteristic drives them to leverage industry challenges into opportunities, paving the way for improved profitability and long-term success. Family enterprises that encourage upskilling *everyone* in the organization ensure they remain abreast of industry trends and future-proof their operations.

4.4 Next-gen committees

To preserve and strengthen family businesses' founding values, it is essential to establish a next-gen committee that fosters innovative approaches to governance while maintaining the organization's core values.

Family enterprises must adapt to changing times and address future scenarios by reevaluating the structure and role of family councils. The committees must have proven effective in communicating fresh ideas that safeguard the interests of future generations.

External enterprises

As family enterprises pivot towards new objectives, partnerships with other companies outside of their immediate circle can provide new growth opportunities.

Family businesses prioritize the development of women in the organization, help open up new avenues for the family enterprise, and provide opportunities for females in the workforce, thus keeping up with the changes in family and global dynamics.

Incorporating the next generation in the family business

When the children become involved in the family business, some common conflicts arise involving entitlement accusations and indifference among non-family members working within a company.

There have been common occurrences where children in the family business might not put in the same hours and are evaluated differently than non-family members. This could sometimes create resentment for non-family members seeking promotions or higher compensation in a family business.

Transition means transformation

Children interested in the family's legacy business and industry are to transition their inclusion into the company, over time. When they reach full-time working age, having your children work elsewhere for at least 2–3 years is best.

This could be with another company in the same industry, an investment banking or business advisory firm within the same industry.

It is a move that forces the next generation to learn accountability and establish a work ethic without the protection of family members. It also allows children to understand the business from different perspectives and perhaps find aspects of the company that work for their personalities.

Preparing the children well makes a meaningful difference when it is time to call them back into the family business.

Anne Klein

If they did outstanding work elsewhere, they would have the professional respect and credibility of the non-family members. This alone makes a big difference moving forward.

For the family business, you bring home a child who has learned new perspectives and gained industry knowledge that can help evolve the family business.

Nonetheless, it is vital to establish formal governance in the family business, specifically for family members working within the company.

Under-performance

A common challenge that should be addressed within family business governance revolves around under-performing family members. This policy must balance key performance metrics and expectations while being transparent about such difficulties as entitlement.

It is also crucial that family values are recognized and identified as values that children working within the family business must adhere to.

Committee with at least one family member

In larger companies, establishing a committee consisting of at least one family member, one employed non-family member, and an independent career-related professional. This allows family-owned businesses to maintain checks and balances involving family members working within the industry.

Committees are not what you think

This committee approach can help establish how to provide **guidance and feedback** involving the development of family members within a family business. It can also help identify **personality conflicts** that can be addressed and adjusted over time between family and non-family members within the industry.

The framework should minimize the need to separate or terminate a family member from the business unless a dire and severe circumstance requires immediate termination.

If separation is the outcome for a family member, it should be performed with dignity, and the family member should be assisted in identifying a career fit elsewhere.

5 Dealing with stress within the family and family office environment

When stress levels remain consistently high, it can hinder teams from performing at their best, as they may find themselves in survival mode and unable to generate innovative solutions. It is important to cultivate an environment where individuals feel mentally, emotionally, and physically secure.

Anne Klein

Dealing with stress and stressful situations within the family and family office environment can be difficult.

5.1 The art of emotional intelligence

Our primary goal is to make a difference. We must carry out our goals and responsibilities without taking on someone else's emotions. It is essential to respect and listen to others without internalizing their feelings. We should not allow others to project their feelings onto us; establishing our boundaries can help reduce stress.

Boundaries

Establish your boundaries and adhere to them. Only take action when necessary, as some people may frequently disregard your personal and professional boundaries, putting you in an uncomfortable position. Communicate your expectations regarding response times and preferred methods of communication with others.

Time management and stress

Apart from its contribution to setting boundaries, organizing your workload effectively help to reduce stress levels. Delegate, and lighten the load with different tools and strategies.

Stay up to speed with your profession and enhance your skills

One works better and faster when one stays up to speed with matters and diligently works towards sustaining and improving one's skills. Surround yourself with good professional networks to help you with the support required to reduce stress levels.

5.2 Stress management

Manage your stress levels and stay true to yourself. Engage in activities that bring you joy and remind you of your purpose.

Evaluate the individuals, situations, and environments contributing to your stress and take proactive steps to address and manage them.

Therapy

Therapy can help you better understand yourself and become the best version of yourself. This is a personal journey; you must manage it with care and respect. There's no need to overshare what you do with others. Seek help if needed and work with professionals who understand the importance of seeking counseling.

Anne Klein

Find your balance

It is important to bring things back into balance. Actively work towards finding your rhythm.

Empowering others

Educating others empowers them to create more supportive environments.

Make your life easier by
educating others on the complexities of
topics and services they dismiss as simple.

Anne Klein

5.3 The power of transformation in family offices

What do you have in place?

The following areas are critical for the effective operation of a family office:

- Utilization of financial reporting software from an external source.
- Establishment and management of the investment committee.
- Documentation of the investment process.
- Implementation of a financial performance measurement process.
- Development of a wealth succession plan for family members.
- Annual budgeting process for the family office.
- Review process for all activities and operations of the family office.
- Annual performance review process for staff members.
- Establishment of job descriptions for all roles covered by the family office.
- Creation and review of a governance framework.
- Implementation of cybersecurity controls.
- Execution of risk management processes beyond investments.
- Development of a family office strategy and operating manual.
- Selection and review of external parties.
- Establishment of a succession plan for the family office.

Family balance sheet and holding structures

The family office must review a detailed description of your assets, business structures, entities, and any trust structures and liabilities.

The founder's wish is to have influence over the family's wealth

Should a client prefer specific duties and responsibilities within the family's wealth framework, strategies could be considered to support the family, such as preparing a detailed **Letter of Wishes** and acting, for example, as a co-director of the asset holding companies.

5.4 How to proceed with the creation of a Family Charter

Let's empower family office representatives with the tools and strategies they need to understand and contribute to the unique family narrative.

Anne Klein

Step one:

Hire an experienced advisor, strictly for governance and drafting the Family Charter. They will cultivate a comprehensive training session covering various aspects, including an introduction to different types of family offices, key concepts and definitions, success stories, and contingency plans to address potential pitfalls.

Step two:

Discussion with the founding family member(s) and advisors: introduction and planning.

Step three:

Training for the next-gen and family (decide who must attend). The training material can be customized to use family logos, quotes, and designs.

⇒ *Creation and customization of training material.*

⇒ *Creation of family training invitation.*

⇒ *Setting the scene document.*

⇒ *Feedback from family before finalization of documents.*

⇒ *Delivery of training.*

Step four:

Create and design a *family questionnaire* and determine the format to be used.

Step five:

Family meeting to discuss the family governance and charter.

Step six:

Ongoing collaboration and design of the Family Charter.

Step seven:

⇒ *Signing ceremony.*

⇒ *Ongoing evolution and implementation of the Family Charter and governance structures.*

LDK ⬆ LDK

Chapter 10

Powerful Purpose for Families and Individuals

A dedication and recognition
to those who created rainbows
for us to enjoy ...

Over the Rainbow

Song by Judy Garland

Lyrics

Somewhere over the rainbow

Way up high

There's a land that I heard of

Once in a lullaby

Somewhere over the rainbow

Skies are blue

And the dreams that you dare to dream

Does come true

Someday, I'll wish upon a star.

And wake up where the clouds are far behind me

Where troubles melt like lemon drops

Away above the chimney tops

That's where you'll find me.

Somewhere over the rainbow

Bluebirds fly

Birds fly over the rainbow

Why then, oh, why can't I?

Somewhere over the rainbow

Bluebirds fly

Birds fly over the rainbow

Why then, oh, why can't I?

If happy little bluebirds fly

Beyond the rainbow

Why, oh why can't I?

1 Finding your inner rainbow

Healing yourself is generational wealth.
Anonymous

1.1 Be the hero of your journey

During the graduation season, people often reach out to others for career advice. If you've recently graduated, here are a few perspectives to help you transition from school to the real world. Firstly, understand that while you may have had big plans when you left school, things may have worked out differently. The sooner you can adjust to this new reality, the better off you will find your brand. Be patient, as success usually takes time to achieve. Keep going even if you do not land your dream job immediately.

1.2 Keep it real

Do not simply chase money or fake job titles when considering job offers. Choose the opportunity that allows you to work with the right people and offers the potential for long-term success. Be open to new experiences, even those that take you out of your comfort zone. You never know what might come of them.

1.3 Continue to seek excellence

While others post on social media, focus on your work and building relationships with influential people. Refrain from accumulating titles; concentrate on gathering experiences, cultivating meaningful connections, and starting by creating sustainable wealth. Remember that you are not competing against anyone else but rather against your potential. Always strive to improve yourself and work towards your next level each day.

Creating more rainbows

*I frequently recommend businesses discuss
creating their own skills training course—
specific to their industry—through social media.*

Brian DeLucia

1.4 Training more talent for skilled jobs

Many people enjoy daily conversations with individuals involved in the traditional business community, such as those related to manufacturing, distribution, business services, logistics, and technology. While discussions may revolve around creating greatness, hiring a more substantial accounting firm, and finding a better fit for the position of CFO, there are now more discussions about the challenges of hiring people to fill technical jobs.

Business owners are now discussing the need for more skilled candidates for these positions.

1.5 Take control of your creativity

Businesses must think outside the box and take initiative. This approach serves as an additional source of revenue for your primary business. It also enables you to connect with potential talent directly, offer industry-specific training, and demonstrate clear pathways for career growth.

This method helps you build a strong talent pool and hire the top candidates you identify. It harnesses the power of modern social media while retaining traditional people skills.

This approach offers job seekers the possibility of securing well-paying jobs without accumulating significant debt — and incredibly enticing prospect in today's economic climate.

2 Into infinity for humanity

The Brand is YOU.

Brian DeLucia

Love Thy Neighbor.

Dr. Martin Luther King

The world may face difficulties, but it is essential to remember that there is still much good. Unfortunately, today, people tend to speak in extremes and allow their emotions to control their actions.

Let us remember the leadership of Dr. Martin Luther King Jr. and his messages of love, education, and peace, which he spread against all obstacles. It is essential to follow the commandment of *"Love Thy Neighbor as You Love Yourself"* which applies to everyone, no matter their faith.

How can we forget something so simple?

It is not *Love Thy Neighbor* unless they are a Conservative.

It is not *Love Thy Neighbor* unless they are Liberal.

It is not *Love Thy Neighbor* unless they are of a different race.

It is not *Love Thy Neighbor* unless they are of a different orientation.

It is not *Love Thy Neighbor* unless they are of a different nationality.

It is not *Love Thy Neighbor* unless they are from the same high school as you.

It is not *Love Thy Neighbor* unless they are fans of the same team.

Love Thy Neighbor as You Love Yourself.

Imagine a world where we practiced something so simple that it could end all the division among us. Let's make this a reality by starting with ourselves and inspiring those around us to do the same.

Let's all spread this philosophy.

It is simple ... your brand is YOU.

Take a moment to reflect on your strengths and consider the unique qualities that make you stand out. Remember that you are a brand, and it's essential to have self-confidence.

While you don't have to be the life of the party, you must be genuine and authentic. Embrace your unique qualities and use them to connect with others.

Remember that starting a conversation can be as simple as saying "hello!"

Would you like to give it a try? It worked in 1980. It will work in 2024+. The technology is just different.

> *A few years ago, I said hello to a long-time financier who began a dialogue series over the past few years.*
>
> *I have connected people with this gentleman, who connected me with two gentlemen in a business partnership. One day, I conversed with these partners about a large project.*
>
> Brian DeLucia

Although it may seem old-fashioned, greeting people can be an effective way to connect with them. Starting a conversation with a simple hello can help establish rapport and build strong relationships.

It's important to remember that everyone has something valuable to offer, regardless of background or experience.

We all bring unique perspectives and skills to the table, and it's essential to recognize and appreciate these contributions.

We have a real-life example of how this works. I am saying hello. Pretty simple.

A group was facing a challenge when someone reached out and said hello. Despite being only 31 years old, he knew his worth. He was then invited to a meeting where he walked into a room, knowing people were skeptical about what this so-called kid could bring. However, within 15 minutes, he owned the meeting and showed how to turn a $200 million project into a reality.

A significant challenge with a $250 million project was solved through a simple conversation.

A simple everyday conversation I had at a Starbucks in August 2016 after I dropped someone a note to say hello.

This simple hello led to a cup of your favorite daytime beverage. As we were building familiarity, this professional mentioned to me a challenge that she, her attorney friend, and her Certified Public Account (CPA) friend had with a business owner who had a significant challenge after losing a major client.

After speaking with her two other colleagues and the business owner in the next few days. We could bring small loans and business development strategies by learning about their situation. It is incredible how saying hello resolves challenges and creates opportunities.

Brian DeLucia

2.1 Find the five-year-old within

Interpersonal communication occurs frequently throughout our daily lives, with each interaction serving a specific purpose. It is essential to strive for meaningful and constructive dialogue in all conversations, even those that may initially appear unimportant. While some discussions may seem quiet or uneventful, they present personal growth opportunities.

Expressing individual eccentricities and quirks is acceptable, as it contributes to one's uniqueness and memorability.

Authenticity and comfort in communication are generally appreciated, whereas attempting to emulate others may lead to negative attention.

Chasing sunsets

Life can be challenging, and it's easy to become bitter. But it's essential to remember that happiness is within us all, just like a happy five-year-old kid. We should embrace that inner child within ourselves and strive to bring joy and positivity to our lives. Sharing our stories and involving others is a great way to engage people.

By creating co-stars in our stories, we can take people along for the ride and make our lives more exciting. Each person, including you, brings something unique to the table.

So, let's make our conversations more constructive and meaningful and embrace our true selves. The story is never about us.

2.2 Twisted truths

Twisted truths can create challenging landscapes. How can you tell if you are in a toxic situation? Sometimes, you may find yourself in a challenging and toxic situation that does not make sense to the logical mind and could cause severe emotional, physical, and financial pain and misfortune.

What are the warning signs?

Several things might make you feel out of alignment with your true nature, but do they make you feel empty? As an empath, align yourself with the right places, people, and opportunities in your personal or professional life, and embrace your special gift.

Empower yourself when you notice some of these elements in your current life, and take steps to change your situation for a better outcome.

When you find yourself in a place where:

♦ Everything happens in extremes; each shared story is always much more gigantic than reality.

♦ Everything is controlled.

♦ Fear is spread like wildfire, from namedropping to negative talk.

♦ Stories always have a negative spin or place a sprinkle of doubt on others.

♦ Drama is made out of nothing.

♦ Emotions are turned on and shut down in an automated fashion as a manipulation tool.

♦ Charm is turned on when a favor is needed.

♦ Isolation is a method of control.

♦ Breadcrumbs are used to manipulate you.

♦ Twisted truths are used for personal gain.

There is more to add to the list, but if any of these elements are present in your life and you do not feel comfortable with them, reflect on what you can do.

2.3 Some of the things that might help you

Speak to a friend, reach out to a professional, think about ways of minimizing your interactions or exposure to the situation, take active steps to align with your true nature, and start working on finding a long-term solution where you can live the life of your dreams with the people, places, and things you love. There is always a way to get to a better place if you acknowledge the situation and take steps to action to create a better future for yourself.

Face your inner obstacles for a better family and life story.

Although we cannot alter the challenges of the past,
collaborative efforts can be directed toward
comprehending and resolving obstacles.
Complementary methodologies and techniques
can address deeply ingrained behavioral patterns
or adverse perceptions hindering attaining
a more enriching and purposeful life.

Dr Susan Roets

LDK ⬤ LDK

Chapter 11

Into the Future and a Recap

It is great to see you again today!

1 Use the following pages to reflect how you wish to experience your future

Family offices can achieve greatness by embracing a fundamental truth: understanding the relationship between "costs" and risk.
By remembering this principle,
family offices can unlock new opportunities that lead to greater success and a brighter future for all.

Brian DeLucia

No limits ...

Big dreams ...

A better today for a brighter tomorrow.

2 The future of artificial intelligence (AI) for families, nextgen

Family enterprises can create new opportunities for the next generation by combining leadership transition with generative AI. A significant shift is underway as a new generation of leaders takes over family-owned businesses.

This transformation is driven by the revolutionary capabilities of Generative AI (GenAI). It marks a change in leadership style and a strategic move towards adopting new technology within family-run establishments.

Embrace AI

For those adept at leveraging it, generative AI holds the potential to influence future success significantly. The forthcoming cohort of family business leaders is pivotal in driving this paradigm shift.

Our comprehensive analysis, encompassing over 900 individuals from NextGen, indicates their heightened optimism towards generative AI compared to the *preceding* generation and their acknowledgment of the pressing necessity to divest AI accountability from isolated compartments, and integrate it to facilitate widespread adoption throughout their organizations.

A striking 73% of NextGen stakeholders perceive generative AI as a potent transformation catalyst, yet many doubt their family businesses' capacity to harness its potential fully.

Generative AI

NextGen shows remarkable alignment with the sentiment of global chief executives regarding the transformative powers of generative AI.

According to the 2024 PwC Global CEO Survey, 70% of business leaders believe that generative AI will significantly change how their business creates, delivers, and captures value.

We also see broad acknowledgment of the importance of developing an "early days" generative AI strategy to get ahead of an accelerating existential crisis. Half of all bosses of privately owned companies — of which family businesses are an essential subset — say that their company will cease viable within ten years if they stay on the current path.

Transition

Family enterprises must acknowledge this transition. Family businesses are a substantial constituent of the global economy, contributing an estimated 70% of the worldwide GDP and employing approximately 60% of the world's workforce. Consequently, the effective utilization of generative AI extends beyond merely sustaining a firm's competitiveness; it is instrumental in shaping the global economic landscape.

As the prospective proprietors and principal beneficiaries of the most substantial wealth transfer in history, the forthcoming generation possesses a distinct obligation toward their businesses, employees, families, society, and the environment. This obligation encompasses a pronounced vested interest in their businesses' capacity to prudently navigate the anticipations, prospects, and apprehensions associated with generative AI.

Critical issues

Three critical areas—innovation, trust, and succession—show that these changes cannot be delayed until the next natural generational ownership transition. They must begin now.

GenAI

Wealth and asset management firms invest in the GenAI era to transform their business models and operations. Potential use cases are prioritized based on their near-term impact on the value chain. However, strong governance models and controls are necessary to address tech risks.

GenAI had a transformative effect on wealth and asset management, with firms investing in use cases that can improve decision-making and efficiency and reduce costs. Wealth managers expect client onboarding, marketing, and acquisition to see significant time and cost savings using GenAI, while asset managers cite onboarding and portfolio management.

Firms acknowledge the importance of strong governance models and controls to ensure the ethical use of GenAI. Adopting GenAI will help wealth and asset managers remain competitive in the financial industry.

The next major step for the field is humanoid robots that do real work, plan out activities, and interact with the physical world in ways that are not just interactions between feet and the ground.

Alan Fern

In a remarkable achievement, researchers have successfully employed an AI technique called reinforcement learning to help a two-legged robot nicknamed Cassie perform various tasks.

Cassie could run 400 meters, execute standing long jumps and high jumps, and navigate varying terrains without being explicitly trained on each movement. This approach allowed the robot to learn how to generalize and respond to new scenarios, thereby avoiding the common problem of freezing up that had plagued previous robots.

It's exciting to see how this technology can help us develop more advanced and adaptable robots in the future.

Due to a fragile self-image,
people might push the boundaries for
time, energy, and attention and
put you in uncomfortable situations.

Anne Klein

Stepping into the future with greater clarity for prosperity

Finally, remember that your words hold power. Honor them. Nothing is personal; assumptions are messy. Give it your all and do your best.

One of the most beautiful qualities of true friendship is
to understand and to be understood.

Lucius Annaeus Seneca

3 A recap of family offices

The *Citi Global Family Office Insights 2023* report reveals that there are 268 single family offices, with 86% belonging to the 1st and 2nd generations. Approximately 50% of these offices manage over US$500 million in assets (AUM). Critical concerns for these offices include inflation, interest rate increases, and US-China relations.

The report also indicates that 77% of family offices with less than US$500 million AUM employ between one to six employees. In comparison, 60% of family offices with more than US$500 million AUM have seven or more employees.

Regarding asset allocation, equity represents 22%, fixed income 16%, real estate 14%, cash equivalents 12%, and private equity funds 12%.

Furthermore, the report highlights the top five *focuses* for family offices:

♦ Wealth management services.

- ◆ Investment management.

- ◆ Operating businesses.

- ◆ Accounting.

- ◆ Fostering family unity and continuity.

The top *concerns* for families and principals are preserving the value of assets, preparing the next generation to be responsible wealth owners, ensuring shared goals and vision for their future, leadership transitions, and strengthening family governance.

An overview of the top five international services reveals reporting, accounting, philanthropy, investment management, and wealth planning. The challenges faced by family offices include adapting to changing market conditions, meeting the needs and expectations of family members, attracting and retaining talent, implementing technology solutions, and navigating regulatory compliance.

For *Family Office Portfolio Management & Investments*, the report indicates that family offices expect portfolio returns to increase by more than +10% (65%), rising between 0% to +10% (30%) or remaining unchanged or decreasing (5%). Moreover, the top five asset class allocations are public equities (22%), fixed income (16%), real estate (14%), cash and cash equivalents (12%), and private equity funds (12%).

The distribution of asset class allocations by region is:

- ⇒ *North America (57%).*

- ⇒ *Europe (16%).*

- ⇒ *APAC ex-China (11%).*

- ⇒ *China (8%).*

- ⇒ *Latin America (7%).*

The most bullish asset classes for family offices are developed investment grade fixed income (45%), private credit (44%), private equity direct (38%), cash (34%), and private equity funds/funds of funds (32%).

On the other hand, the most bearish asset classes are crypto assets (49%), real estate (32%), developed corporate high-yield fixed income (27%), emerging market fixed income (25%), and hedge funds (25%).

For future asset allocations, family offices plan to increase their investments in technology (69%), healthcare (58%), energy (28%), real estate (28%), and financials (27%).

When it comes to private equity allocations, family offices favor growth equity (30%), venture capital (27%), buyout (19%), funds of funds (8%), and secondary (6%).

Direct investments are preferred by 80% of family offices, while 20% do not favor them. The top sources of deal flow include internal teams (51%), other families or family offices (49%), networking groups/investment clubs (36%), investment advisors (24%), and banks (21%).

Results also indicate that 72% of family offices have sustainable investment allocations, while 28% do not. Additionally, 61% of portfolio assets are managed in-house, and external investment managers manage 39%.

Sixty-four percent of family offices have investment committees, 10% are in the process of establishing one, and 26% do not have an investment committee. Finally, family offices' top five philanthropic focuses are education, healthcare and medical research, the arts, civil and societal benefits, and youth development.

4 Africa wealth landscape

Forbes has published a list of the top 15 most powerful and wealthiest families in South Africa, which was determined by tracking the net worth of both individuals and families.

Rank	Family	Net Worth
1	Johann Rupert and family	US$11.4 billion
2	Nicky Oppenheimer and family	US$9.4 billion
3	Ivan Glasenberg and family	US$8 billion
4	Koos Bekker and family	US$2.7 billion
5	Douw Steyn and family	US$2.647 billion
6	Patrice Motsepe and family	US$2.6 billion
7	Allan Gray family	US$1.8 billion
8	Michiel Le Roux and family	US$1.2 billion
9	Christo Wiese and family	US$1.2 billion

10	Stephen Bradley Saad and family	US$1.2 billion
11	Christoffel Wiese and family	US$1.2 billion
12	Jannie Mouton and family	US$1 billion
13	Lauritz Dippenaar and family	US$610 million
14	Raymond Ackerman and family	US$500 million
15	Adrian Gore and family	US$480 million

The *AfrAsia Bank Africa Wealth Report 2021,* in partnership with *New World Wealth*, presents a detailed analysis of the wealth industry in Africa. It highlights the impact of COVID-19 on the continent and recent luxury and wealth management trends.

Ranks by city of millionaires, 2022

1. New York City
2. Tokyo
3. San Francisco Bay Area
4. London
5. Singapore
6. Los Angeles
7. Hong Kong
8. Beijing
9. Shanghai
10. Sydney

LDK — LDK

Migration of HNWIs by country

The following table shows the countries with the highest net inflows and outflows of HNWIs in 2023, according to the annual *Henley & Partners Wealth Migration Report*. Figures have been rounded to the nearest 100.

Incoming HNWIs 2023

Rank	Country	No. of Inflow
1	Australia	5,200
2	United Arab Emirates	4,500
3	Singapore	3,200
4	United States of America	2,100
5	Switzerland	1,800

List of considerations

Here are some factors that families and advisors should consider:

Tax planning for internal restructurings, such as legal entity rationalization and value chain management.

Assistance with intellectual property and cash access planning.

Tax planning services for cross-border mergers, acquisitions, and disposition transactions.

Support for international tax dispute resolution.

Assistance with international tax reporting and compliance.

Provision of international tax support for financial reporting.

Tax modeling and computational services to help with your tax calculations and planning.

Ideas for your Personal /Family Business Values

Choose your values ...

Acceptance	Accomplishment	Accountability
Accuracy	Achievement	Adaptability
Alertness	Altruism	Ambition
Ambitiousness	Amusement	Assertiveness
Attentive	Authority	Awareness
Balance	Balance of work	Beauty
Becoming an expert	Boldness	Bravery
Brilliance	Calm	Candor
Capable	Careful	Certainty
Challenge	Charity	Cleanliness
Clear	Clever	Collaboration
Comfort	Commitment	Commitment to excellence
Common sense	Communication	Community
Compassion	Competence	Concentration
Confidence	Connection	Consciousness
Consistency	Contentment	Continuous Learning
Contribution	Control	Conviction
Cooperation	Courage	Courtesy
Creation	Creativity	Credibility
Curiosity	Daring	Decisiveness
Dedication	Dependability	Determination
Develop professional networks	Development	Devotion
Dignity	Discipline	Discovery
Diversity	Drive	Effectiveness
Efficiency	Empathy	Empower
Endurance	Energy	Enjoyment
Enthusiasm	Equality	Ethical
Excellence	Experience	Exploration
Expressive	Fairness	Family
Family security	Famous	Fearless
Feelings	Ferocious	Fidelity
Flexibility	Focus	Foresight
Forgiving	Fortitude	Freedom
Freedom	Friendship	Fun
Generosity	Genius	Giving
Going above and beyond	Goodness	Grace security
Gratitude	Greatness	Growth

Growth mindset	Happiness	Hard work
Harmony	Health	Honesty
Honor	Honoring commitments	Hope
Humble	Humility	Humor
Imagination	Improvement	Inclusivity
Independence	Individuality	Innovation
Inquisitive	Insightful	Inspiring
Integrity	Intelligence	Intensity
Intuitive	Joy	Justice
Kindness	Knowledge	Lawfultemperance
Leadership	Learning	Liberty
Life	Listening to customers	Logic
Love	Loyalty	Mastery
Maturity	Meaning	Moderate
Moderation	Motivation	Obedient
Objectivity	Open-mindedness	Openness
Optimism	Order uniqueness	Organization unity
Originality	Passion	Patience
Peace	Performance	Persistence
Playfulness	Poise	Positive attitude
Positivity	Potential	Power
Present	Proactivity	Problem-solving
Productivity	Professionalism	Prosperity
Protecting the environment	Punctuality	Purpose
Pursuing growth opportunities	Quality	Quality of Service
Realistic	Reason	Recognition
Recreation	Reflective	Reliability
Resourcefulness	Respect	Respect and integrity
Respect for individuality	Respect for privacy	Responsibility
Restraint	Results-oriented	Reverence
Rigor	Satisfaction	Self-awareness
Self-improvement	Selfless	Self-reliance
Self-respect	Sense of belonging	Sensitivity
Serenity	Service	Sharing
Significance	Silence	Simplicity
Sincerity	Skill	Skillfulness
Smart	Social justice	Social order

Social power	Social recognition	Solitude
Solution focused	Spirit	Spiritual life
Spirituality	Spontaneous	Stability
Status	Stewardship	Strength
Structure	Success	Support
Surprise	Sustainability	Talent
Teamwork	Thankful	Thorough
Thoughtful	Timeliness	Tolerance
Toughness	Traditional	Tranquility
Transparency	Trust	Trustworthy
Truth	Understanding	Unity
Valor	Victory	Vigor
Vision	Vitality	Wealth
Welcoming	Willingness to Learn	Winning
Wisdom	Wonder	

Add your three top values below:

What are your shared values?:

Family Charter

Values	Vision	Mission	Definition
Ownership	Employment	Communication	Values

Annexures

Abbreviations
Definitions
Bibliography

I Global tax transparency abbreviations and definitions that will assist with your view on compliance

AEOI	Automatic Exchange of Information.
CARF	Crypto-Asset Reporting Framework.
Controlling person	Settlor, Trustee, Protector, Beneficiaries or class of Beneficiaries, or any other natural person exercising ultimate effective control over a Trust.
CRS	Common Reporting Standard. The Common Reporting Standard (CRS) and the United States Foreign Account Tax Compliance Act ("FATCA") changed tax reporting worldwide.
De minimis	is Latin for "of minimum importance."
FATCA	Foreign Account Tax Compliance Act.
FFI	Foreign Financial Institution.
FTI	Foreign Taxpayer Information.

GIIN	Global Intermediary Identification Number.
IGA	Intergovernmental Agreement.
Indicia	Identifying characteristics/qualities.
KYC	Know-your-client.
NFFE & NPFI	Non-Financial Foreign Entity & Non-Participating
RO	Reporting Officer
Specified Reportable Person	Individual or legal entity with a reportable account.
Sponsoring Entity	A Legal Entity that undertakes the reporting obligations on behalf of a sponsored entity.
TIN	Taxpayer Identification Number
VDP	Voluntary Disclosure Program

This is a partial list; the terminology is mainly based on US terminology. It is essential to obtain expert advice on reporting obligations.

2 Types of family offices

Single Family Office (SFO/FO)

A single family office is a comprehensive wealth management solution for affluent individuals or families seeking a personalized approach to managing their wealth. This type of service provides a full-balance-sheet approach that caters to the client's unique financial needs and objectives. With a single family office, clients can enjoy a holistic approach to wealth management that prioritizes their economic well-being.

Virtual Family Office

For exceptionally wealthy individuals and families, the single family office is often the preferred method of managing their financial and personal affairs. The single family office offers expertise in wealth management, including investment management and wealth planning, as well as support services such as administrative and lifestyle services and special projects.

The virtual family office, on the other hand, is a more accessible alternative. It offers similar benefits to a single family office but is designed to cater to a broader range of families.

It achieves this by providing a synergistic approach and extensive expertise, all while utilizing technology and collaboration through cloud-based solutions.

Multi-Family Office (MFO)

A multi-family office may best serve individuals and families with over US$20 million in assets. Multi-family offices allow families to access the benefits of a dedicated single family office without the overhead and responsibility of running a new business.

Embedded Family Office

An embedded family office is a unique type of family office. It refers to a group of staff working within a family business who are responsible for managing the private assets and needs of the business owners. They also handle the company's business management, including finance and operations. Embedded family offices have become necessary because, historically, most wealth is generated through family businesses. Once a company becomes successful and generates excess cash, its owners must manage it and its earnings effectively.

3 General definitions that family offices and estate planning advisors use

The Absolute Return

Absolute return is the percentage change in the value of an asset over a specific period. It only measures the performance of a particular investment and doesn't compare it to any benchmark.

Accredited Investor

An accredited investor is an individual or a business entity allowed to trade securities that may not be registered with financial authorities. They are entitled to this privileged access by satisfying at least one requirement regarding their income, net worth, asset size, governance status, or professional experience.

Accretion-Dilution Analysis

An accretion/dilution analysis is a simple test to evaluate the merit of a proposed merger or acquisition deal. It determines whether the accretion/dilution analysis is a straightforward method for estimating the value of a proposed merger or acquisition.

It assesses whether the earnings per share (EPS) increase or decrease after the transaction. Post-transaction earnings per share (EPS) will increase or decrease.

Alpha

Alpha refers to an investment's excess return over a benchmark index's return.

Alpha can be positive or negative, indicating outperformance or underperformance, respectively, compared to the benchmark.

Asset Allocation

Asset allocation involves diversifying investments among assets with different correlations to reduce portfolio volatility.

Asset protection

Specific techniques can be used to minimize risk; each jurisdiction has different rules, regulations, and structures that can be used. The list is not exhaustive:

Limited liability companies.

Companies are limited by guarantee.

Protected Cell Companies.

Contractual arrangements such as an option or an agency.

Contractual relationships relating to possession.

Various pour-over devices, whereby assets and rights can be moved.

Foundations.

Assets Under Management (AUM)

AUM refers to the market value of investments that a person or entity manages on behalf of clients. When assessing a company, AUM is considered alongside management performance and experience. Some financial institutions calculate AUM by including bank deposits, mutual funds, and cash, while others only consider funds under discretionary management from individual investors.

Beta Market Risk

Market risk, or systematic risk or beta, refers to the volatility in prices in the equity and bond markets from broad economic influences or events. This type of risk cannot be eliminated through diversification.

Board of Advisors

Many businesses, including family offices, have a group of trusted advisors from related industries. However, if a family office puts effort into building a diverse and strong board of advisors, they will benefit from having such a valuable resource in place.

Capital draw down

The company and the holders mutually decide the terms, including interest rate, maturity date, repayment, and amortization schedule (if any), for each working capital note before the applicable working capital drawdown date.

Capital Raising Consultant

A capital-raising consultant is someone whose primary goal is to help a company raise money. Their work typically involves creating materials to attract investors, such as a teaser or executive summary, a business plan and placement memorandum, and a management presentation (also known as a pitch deck). They may also prepare financial projections, models, and valuation analyses and manage a data room.

Additionally, fundraising consultants can assist with defining the investor pool, reaching out to potential investors, reviewing term sheets, and documenting final deal terms. They may help management develop a strategy and implement business development initiatives to make the company more attractive to investors.

Centi-millionaires

Individuals with investable wealth of US$100 million or more.

Claw-Back Provision

Claw-back is a provision in which employees return incentive-based pay, such as bonuses, to their employer with a penalty.

Commodities

A commodity is a raw material or primary agricultural product that can be bought and sold. Commodities are often used as inputs in producing other goods or services.

Corporate Sustainability Reporting

Companies must prioritize sustainability in decision-making, giving them a competitive advantage. Understanding the future of any reporting requirements is essential.

Debt Recapitalization

A debt recapitalization strategy allows business owners to withdraw cash from their company while reducing their investment risk by transferring it to other assets. To do this, an outside financing source provides debt capital through senior and mezzanine debt, which can then be distributed to the owners as cash.

Derivatives

A derivative is an agreement whose value is based on the performance of an underlying asset, such as a commodity, stock, or currency. Derivatives can be used to hedge against risk and for speculative purposes.

Directional and Non-Directional Risks

Directional risk is the potential loss due to the exposure to a specific market's assets. For example, if an investor owns shares in a company and the market price of those shares decreases, the investor will experience a loss. On the other hand, non-directional risk happens when a trader needs to follow their trading strategy consistently.

Discounted Cash Flow Analysis

Discounted cash flow analysis determines the current value of expected future cash flows using a discount rate. It helps investors evaluate whether an investment or project's future cash flows are more significant than its initial value.

Double Taxation Agreement

Several double tax agreements provide for the allocation and taxing rights between the country of income source and the country of residence.

Due Diligence On A Company

Family offices should conduct thorough due diligence when considering investing in a company. This process involves comparing the company's reality with its business plan and taking at least 40 hours to execute. This ensures that decisions are made only after adequately investigating the offering and the team behind the company. Family offices must have policies and processes that enforce this level of due diligence to make informed investment decisions.

Due Diligence

This is a method of gaining knowledge about a business. It also reveals any potential issues that may cause problems in the future. While contractual warranties, representations, and indemnities are in place to protect you, legal remedies often need to be revised or too late.

It is always advisable to make your deal subject to satisfactory due diligence. You can either walk away or negotiate a lower price if you find something uncomfortable. You can use a due diligence questionnaire (DDQ) to conduct due diligence.

Earnings Before Interest, Taxes, Depreciation, And Amortization (EBITDA)

EBITDA, or earnings before interest, taxes, depreciation, and amortization, is an alternate measure of profitability to net income. EBITDA attempts to represent the cash profit generated by the company's operations and includes depreciation, amortization, taxes, and debt payment costs.

Emerging Fund Manager

Emerging managers are typically defined as newly formed or relatively small firms.

Enforcer

An enforcer is a third party in a trust who is not a trustee or beneficiary. This person can be appointed under the trust instrument to ensure the trust's execution. This role is recognized in some jurisdictions.

A Fund Of Funds (FOF)

It is an investment strategy in which one holds a portfolio of other investment funds rather than investing directly in stocks, bonds, or other securities. This type of investment is often referred to as a multi-manager investment.

Forced Heirship

Forced heirship is a legal provision, applicable to certain countries, that restricts how the estator can bequeath their estate under certain conditions.

Foundation

An independent legal entity holding assets for beneficiaries and separately from the personal property of its founder. It is helpful for legacy planning and charitable purposes. Its charter and by-laws govern it, and council members manage it.

Why Do They Use Foundations In Certain Jurisdictions?

It is a separate legal entity; it holds ownership, which is more appropriate for managing and investing in riskier asset classes.

General Partner

A general partner is one of the co-owners of an unincorporated business (organized as a general partnership) who controls the firm. Unlike a limited or nominal partner, a general partner has unlimited personal liability for the firm's debts.

Actions taken by one general partner are binding upon the other general partners. A general partner is also called a full partner.

Global Macro Hedge Fund Strategy

A global macro strategy is an investment and trading strategy based on significant national, regional, and international macroeconomic events. To successfully implement a global macro strategy, analyze various macroeconomic and geopolitical factors. These include interest rates, currency exchange rates, levels of international trade, political events, and international relations. Hard assets range from commodity plays like investing in a copper mine to more run-of-the-mill allocations in a real estate development project.

Hedge Fund

A hedge fund uses various techniques to reduce its exposure to market risk. The goal of a hedge fund manager is to have the fund perform independently of market fluctuations rather than being bound by the traditional stock and bond markets. However, access to hedge funds is often limited to accredited investors, who must meet specific financial criteria and be willing to invest large sums of money. Hedge funds also offer limited liquidity with withdrawal restrictions, making it difficult for investors to cash out their investments quickly.

Additionally, hedge funds are less transparent and highly regulated than public securities such as mutual funds and Stocks. As a result, the tax treatment of hedge fund investments can be complex and may come with significant short-term gain tax liability.

Hedging Risk

Hedging is a strategy for reducing exposure to investment risk. An investor can hedge the risk of one investment by taking an offsetting position in another investment. The values of the offsetting investments should be inversely correlated. Hedge your bet. When an investor buys a stock, he will profit if that stock goes up in value.

High-Watermark

A high-water mark is the highest value an investment account or fund has reached. It is often used as a demarcation point in determining an investor's performance fees.

Hurdle Rate

A hurdle rate is the minimum rate of return that a project or investment must achieve to be profitable. Hurdle rates help companies evaluate whether they should pursue a specific project or investment opportunity. Typically, the riskier the project, the higher the hurdle rate, while less risky projects have lower rates.

Illiquid Assets and Liquid Assets

These assets are more complex to value accurately because of few comparable sales. Because the market for these assets is scarcer, determining the value of needs to berate planning and passing these assets on to descendants is more complicated. Income tax services included within a prime brokerage bundle may include cash management, securities lending, and more.

Marital Regime/Relationship Status

Marriage involves making commitments to each other, and the matrimonial regime establishes the rules for the relationship between spouses. By signing a marriage contract before the wedding, the future spouses can precisely define the property relations during the marriage, determine what happens to the property, and decide on the benefits given to each spouse.

Sometimes, the spouses are subject to the joint ownership system without realizing it. Understanding the marital laws before marriage and speaking with an expert for guidance is essential. If you're in a cohabitation relationship, it's also necessary to understand the potential consequences of this arrangement.

Furthermore, in some countries, your marital regime can be changed after the marriage through a court application, but this could be costly and time-consuming.

Some families have specific marital regime preferences for their family members and discuss and capture this in their family governance documents. Although it might not be binding, it is essential from a family wealth protection perspective.

Public Offering Institutional Investor

Internal rate of return is the annual yield on a private equity investment.

Investment Banking

Investment banking is a division of banking that plays a crucial role in helping individuals and organizations raise capital for various financial activities such as mergers, acquisitions, and public offerings.

Additionally, it provides expert financial advisory services to support clients in making informed decisions about their investments and economic strategies.

Leverage

Leverage can be utilized by borrowing money to invest, which has the potential to magnify both gains and losses.

Probate

Probate validates a will, if one exists, and establishes who can manage the deceased's estate. Before the next of kin or the designated executor can access, transfer, sell, or distribute any of the deceased person's assets, they may need to seek a grant of probate.

What is a Grant of Probate?

A grant of probate is a legal document that may be required to access bank accounts, sell assets, and settle debts after an individual has passed away.

Potential Gains and Losses

When the current price of an asset rises above what an investor pays, it results in a gain. On the other hand, a loss happens when the price drops below the initial investment. A gain is an increase in the value of an asset, while a loss refers to a decrease in value.

Leveraged buyout

A leveraged buyout (LBO) is acquiring another company using a significant amount of borrowed money (bonds or loans) to meet the acquisition cost. The assets of the company being acquired are often used as collateral for the loans and the acquiring company's assets.

Limited Liability Corporation

A Long-short strategy is a hedging practice that the investment manager chooses.

Stocks that perform poorly and use leverage to sell those stocks short. The cash proceeds from selling the stocks short are dividend purchase stocks that outperform the market. When implemented successfully, the investor benefits from stocks (sold short) that are falling in price and stocks (bought long) that are appreciating. A typical example of a long-short portfolio is a 130-30 strategy that involves buying stocks long for 130% of the portfolio and selling stocks short for 30%.

Limited Partner

Here is a brief overview of the family-limited partnership. A family limited partnership is a legal entity with general and limited partners. A family limited partnership is like a limited liability company (LLC). The family limited partnership for management holds investment or business assets. Family members own shares of the partnership and can transition wealth between generations by gifting or transferring shares.

The general partners (usually the parents) have the most control but also fully bear the liabilities. In contrast, limited partners (usually the next generation) have little power and are not responsible for liabilities.

Family limited partnership shares owned by the deceased are included in the taxable estate; however, shares are discounted in value because of their illiquid nature. The discounted valuation reduces the taxable estate's size and transfer taxes due when gifting or bequeathing shares to heirs. Generation-skipping transfer taxes may apply when shares are transferred to a skip generation. Shareholders must also pay income taxes on their portion of partnership income.

Limited Partnership Agreement

If the fund manager grants co-investment rights, the LPA will disclose it. Co-investment agreements may have specific carve-outs. The concept of a lock-up period is crucial for investors in hedge funds and IPOs. During this predetermined duration, investors are prohibited from selling or redeeming their shares. This restriction enables managers to allocate funds to illiquid assets such as privately held businesses or real estate. As such, implementing a lock-up period is customary in the context of hedge funds and initial public offerings (IPOs).

Long-Short Hedge Fund Strategy

Long-short hedge strategy definition: This strategy is a form of hedging where the investment manager selects stocks expected to perform poorly. These stocks are then sold short using leverage. The cash generated from the short sale is reinvested in stocks anticipated to outperform the market. The strategy is successful when the investor benefits from the shorted stocks' falling prices and the long stocks' appreciation. A typical example of a long-short portfolio is a 130-30 strategy, which involves buying stocks long for 130% of the portfolio and selling stocks short for 30%.

Management Buyout

Institutional Buyout definition: An institutional buyout is a strategic move that involves outside institutional investors, such as private equity firms, venture capitalists, or ultra-high-net-worth investors, taking ownership of a company. The buyout is usually intended to be short-term and profitable for the investor, showcasing the strategic thinking and planning involved in such transactions.

Management Fee

Family offices have successfully induced managers to lower fees, with some claiming single-digit performance fees (quite different from the industry standard of 20%). This is an essential shift in the LP-GP structure as investors gain the upper hand, in some cases over capital-hungry managers who are willing to slice fees to attract family office investors.

Master Limited Partnership

A master limited partnership benefits from the favorable tax treatment of limited partnerships and the liquidity of publicly traded securities. A limited partner investor provides capital and receives income from cashflows but is not involved with management decisions. A general partner manages the business operations and receives a fee based on performance. To qualify as a master limited partnership, the business must be primarily involved with real estate, commodities, or natural resources.

Maximum Drawdown

Merger arbitrage hedge fund strategy merger arbitrage is an event-driven hedging strategy that involves buying long and selling short the stocks of companies engaged in merger and acquisition deals. The targeted companies are bought long after trading below the acquisition price.

The acquired company is sold shortly before the price drops to reflect the amount paid for the deal. If the agreement is not completed for any reason or is disapproved of, prices can move in the wrong direction on either side of the transaction and negatively impact performance.

Mergers and Acquisitions

Prime brokerage refers to a bundle of services investment banks and other major financial institutions offer to hedge funds and similar clients.

Mezzanine Financing

Mezzanine financing is financing that has both features of debt and equity.

Financing that provides lender risk-adjusted to convert their loan into equity in case of a default (only after other senior debts are paid off)

MOPPSCABE

Market opportunities for profitable products or services with competitive advantages and barriers to E, try a multi-family office. Individuals and families with assets greater than US$20 million may be best served by an MFO.

MFOs allow families to access the benefits of a dedicated single family office without the overhead and responsibility of running a new business.

Net present value

Net present value (NPV) is the difference between cash inflows' present value and cash outflows' present value over time. NPV is used in capital budgeting and investment.

NextGen

A group of business-owning family members aged between 18 and early 40s aiming to become responsible owners, influential board members, or visionary leaders.

Non-Accredited Investor

A non-accredited investor does not meet the qualifications of an accredited investor in terms of net worth or annual income. The Securities and Exchange Commission regulates investments intended primarily for non-accredited investors.

Onshore And Offshore Trust Structures For Multi-Generational Wealth

Establishing and utilizing onshore and offshore trust structures can create, increase, and preserve intergenerational wealth. However, it is crucial to work with an expert proficient in the country where the trust is established or domiciled, where the beneficiaries are responsible for taxes, and where the offshore trust jurisdiction is. The choice of jurisdictions should be carefully considered to meet the family's specific needs. Families need to seek advice from professionals with expertise in tax and regulatory requirements, asset holdings, succession planning, ongoing tax implications, and other aspects related to the reporting and responsibilities of the settlor, founder, trustee, economic funder, donor, protector, and trust beneficiaries. Consulting trust and tax experts can help families understand the impact of trust structure on assets, growth, income earned, capital distributions or growth, and funding methods. Moreover, these experts play a crucial role in guiding loans and donations and the comprehensive management and oversight of the trust, ensuring its long-term success.

Offshore vs Onshore Fund Structure

Onshore funds are established in the investor's domestic location and regulated by local governing bodies. They usually are easily accessible and generally inspire high confidence among investors. On the other hand, offshore funds are investments made in locations outside of the investor's domestic jurisdiction and could be spread globally. Typically, high-net-worth individuals and companies invest in offshore funds to access a diverse portfolio.

Operational Due Diligence

Operational due diligence entails thoroughly examining the target's business model and operations to confirm their compatibility with the buyer. This involves assessing all operating processes, supply chain, logistics, procurement, and in-house and departmental efficiencies.

Options

Options are derivative securities bought and sold to give holders the right (but not an obligation) to trade stocks at a specified price during the option's term. The holder may exercise their right or let the option expire without action at the end of the term; however, the seller of an option is obligated to trade. Per the contract, if the holder chooses to act. Calls and puts are two types of options.

Performance Fee

Family offices have successfully induced managers to lower fees, with some claiming single-digit performance fees (quite different from the industry standard of 20%). This is an essential shift in the LP-GP structure as investors gain the upper hand, in some cases over capital-hungry managers who are willing to slice fees to attract family office investors.

Philanthropic Management

When considering getting involved in philanthropy or charitable activities, whether as an individual, family, community group, business, or workplace, it's important to remember that the power to make a difference is in your hands.

It's crucial to explore the various available avenues, as each one offers unique opportunities for impact.

Creating philanthropic structures that align with your values is essential and can pave the way for continuous and meaningful support of charitable causes that are important to you. It's important to consider that the type of philanthropic structure you establish will impact your legal, financial, and operational responsibilities and associated costs. Seeking professional support and tax advice is critical to realizing your vision.

Philanthropists

A philanthropist donates time, money, experience, skills, or talent to improve the world, regardless of status or net worth.

Pitch Deck

Securing venture capital funding:

- Define your company's purpose.
- What problem are you solving?
- What solution do you propose?
- Why is now the right time for your solution?
- Map the market and identify your target audience.
- What sets you apart from your competitors?
- Describe your product in detail.
- Explain your business model.
- Showcase your team.

Prime Brokerage

A prime brokerage is a bundled group of services that investment banks and other financial institutions offer to hedge funds and other large investment clients that need to be able to borrow securities or cash to engage in netting to achieve absolute returns.

Private Investment in Public Equity Private Equity

Private equity refers to investments in non-publicly traded businesses. These deals are usually only available to accredited or institutional investors and are considered illiquid. They require significant capital investments and strict lock-up periods.

Private Placement

A private placement investment opportunity is unavailable to the general public. Because the deal is only offered to select individuals, the capital requirement is high, a prospectus may not be available, and the agreement needs to be Registered with the SEC.

Private Placement Memorandum

Qualitative analysis qualitative research involves collecting and evaluating non-numerical data to understand concepts or subjective opinions. Quantitative research involves collecting and evaluating numerical data. This article discusses qualitative and quantitative research, how they are different, and how they are used in psychology research.

Protected Cell Companies

A protected cell company (PCC) is a corporate structure in which a single legal entity consists of a core linked to several cells with separate assets and liabilities. The central core organization is related to individual cells. Each cell is independent of the other and the company's core, but the entire unit is still a single legal entity. A PCC is sometimes referred to as a segregated portfolio company.

Quantitative Analysis

Quantitative analysis (QA) encompasses a set of methodologies employed to comprehend the dynamics of financial markets and facilitate more astute investment or trading choices. This discipline entails the application of mathematical and statistical tools to scrutinize financial data.

Real Estate Investment Trusts (REITs)

Real estate is one way family offices invest their money. One popular investment vehicle for real estate is a real estate investment trust (REIT). A REIT investment company invests in properties or mortgages and provides an income component. REITs are traded on exchanges like stocks and bonds, making it easy to invest in real estate.

Publicly available REITs typically invest in commercial real estate, such as apartments, hotels, shopping malls, office complexes, and storage units. REIT allow investors to invest in real estate without managing the property themselves.

Discuss with your advisor the tax impact of this structure as it is often a crucial aspect for investors. Real estate investment firms like REITs are popular investment options for family offices.

Registered Investment Advisor

If you need clarification on a specific ruling or law, seeking clarity and ensuring that you comply with all applicable regulations is essential. Consulting with qualified counsel is highly recommended before changing your Family Office or serving non-family clients.

Double-checking that you're operating legally is always a promising idea, even if you make structural or business changes.

Relative Returns

Relative return is the difference between an asset's return and a benchmark over time, also known as alpha in active portfolio management.

Relative Value Hedge

Fund strategy relative value, also called arbitrage strategies, are trading strategies that exploit mispricing in the financial markets among the constant or related assets. Relative value trading is a popular investment strategy among hedge funds.

Managers who try to achieve high returns while minimizing risk. To capitalize on the mispricing of assets, investment managers take long positions in the undervalued and short positions in the overvalued assets with the expectation that prices will revert to their fundamental values.

Managers construct market-neutral portfolios to eliminate systematic risk when using relative value strategies.

Fund managers employ leverage to maximize the low returns that individual trades yield. Relative value funds are an attractive investment for individuals seeking to diversify their portfolios with assets that are uncorrelated with the broader market.

Securities

The concept of "security" encompasses many investment vehicles, including stocks, bonds, notes, debentures, limited partnership interests, oil and gas interests, and investment contracts.

Generally, an investment qualifies as a security if money is invested in a business with the expectation of deriving profits through the efforts of someone other than the investor. Conversely, the following do not fall under the definition of security:

- Currency

- Checks (certified or otherwise), drafts, bills of exchange, or bank letters of credit

- Notes or other instruments reflecting indebtedness arising from mercantile or consumer transactions rather than investment activities

- Interests in deposit accounts with banks or savings and loan associations

- Insurance policies, endowment policies, or annuity contracts wherein an insurance company commits to making payments either as a lump sum or periodically for the duration of a life or a specified period.

Seed Capital

Seed capital is the initial money required to start a new business. The initial funding needed to start the operations of a new business is termed seed capital.

Service Provider Selection Risk

Since most of the operations and the investment team are outsourced, your ability to select the right service providers at the right price is critical.

This comes back to creating your family office compass first, knowing where you are headed, what the mission of the family office is, and having the right experienced and well-connected advisory board constructed so that you can review the most well-qualified service providers instead of the ones who live in your city, or are family friends, etc.

Sharpe Ratio

The Sharpe Ratio is a measure that evaluates performance of an investment by considering its return, and the level of risk associated with that return.

It is a quantitative representation of the concept that higher returns over a specific time period may indicate increased volatility and risk, rather than superior investment expertise.

Sortino Ratio

The formula for calculating the Sortino Ratio is: Sortino Ratio = (Average Realized Return - Expected Rate of Return) / Downside Risk Deviation. The average realized return refers to the weighted mean return of all the investments in an individual portfolio.

Stocks

A stock denotes a proportionate share in the ownership of a company, entitling the holder to a claim on the company's earnings and assets. Consequently, stockholders assume partial ownership of the company. Fluctuations in the value of the business correspondingly impact the value of the stock.

Sukuk

Sukuk is about the finance provider owning tangible assets and earning a return sourced from those assets. This contrasts with conventional bonds, where the investor has a debt instrument earning the return predominantly via interest payment (riba).

Traditional Investments

Traditional investments offer high liquidity because they are easily tradable in the open market. On the other hand, alternative investments tend to have lower liquidity due to lock-up periods or the nature of the asset class, requiring a longer investment horizon.

UCITS 'Undertakings for Collective Investment in Transferable Securities.'

UCITS is a regulatory framework that allows for the sale of cross-boundary mutual funds for EU member states. UCITS gave retail investors transparent, regulated, and cross-border investment opportunities.

Ultra-high net worth and High-net-worth

A high-net-worth individual (HNWI) is used in the financial industry to describe people with liquid assets worth a certain amount. Typically, HNWIs have financial assets (excluding their primary residence) valued over US$1 million.

A very-high-net-worth individual (VHNWI) refers to someone with a net worth of at least US$5 million, and an ultra-high-net-worth individual (UHNWI) has investible assets worth at least US$30 million (adjusted for inflation). People with a net worth of over US$1 billion are in a particular category of UHNWIs.

These categories are widely used in studies of wealth inequality, government regulation, investment suitability requirements, marketing, financing standards, and general corporate strategy.

Valuation

Valuation is the analytical process of determining an asset or company's current (or projected) worth. Various techniques are used for valuation.

Venture Capital

Families don't just make occasional venture capital investments; they operate full-fledged venture capital firms.

Wealth Management

Wealth management encompasses investment, tax, and estate planning, not just investment advice.

References and resources

UBS Global Family Office Report 2024.

Source: PwC's Global NextGen Survey 2024.

LinkedIn's 2024 Most In-Demand Skills.

The Global Manual for Family Offices», Volume 1, Chapter 2.3.5, Pg. 104.
http://amazon.com/author/fulvio-graziotto

«The Global Manual for Family Offices», Volume 1, Chapter 2.3.5, Pg. 108.
http://amazon.com/author/fulvio-graziotto

This 5-second test to expose a narcissist, YouTube, Meadow Devor.

Private Wealth: A summary of our service offering to local and international private clients, PWC.

The Most Memorable Batman Quotes From Every Live-Action Batman ... - Looper

UBS in its latest "Billionaire Ambitions" report.

Source: UBS Global Wealth Report 2023.

Caproasia.com

YouTube: 33 Things Billionaires Believe VYBO

The Single-Family Office book by Richard C. Wilson.

The World's Wealthiest Cities Report 2023 by Henley & Partners.

UBS Billionaire Ambitions Report 2023: The Great Wealth Transfer.

Dentons.com

2023 Global Family Office Compensation Benchmark Report.

https://www.oxfordreference.com/display/10.1093/acref/9780198802525.001.0001/acref-9780198802525-e-4678

https://www.co-oplegalservices.co.uk/probate-solicitors/what-is-probate/

https://andsimple.co/insights/family-offices-europe/

https://www.forbes.com/sites/paulwestall/2024/02/28/what-does-a-family-office-in-the-middle-east-look-like/?sh=bcbefa05cedd

https://www.ubs.com/global/en/family-office-uhnw/reports/billionaire-ambitions-report-2023.html

https://www.forbes.com/sites/paulwestall/2023/11/15/what-does-a-family-office-in-the-usa-look-like/?sh=7749203e2a19

https://www.mentalfloss.com/posts/astor-family-facts.

https://superherojacked.com/2022/02/03/batman-quotes/

https://www.nbcnews.com/better/money/massive-wealth-transfer-could-be-windfall-charities-n124496

https://parade.com/1100530/marynliles/african-proverbs/

https://www.brainyquote.com/quotes/arthur_balfour_165580

https://www.mondly.com/blog/cool-latin-phrases/

https://www.scmp.com/presented/business/topics/defining-family-office-landscape/article/3076156/asian-family-office

https://www.linkedin.com/pulse/evolution-family-offices-response-modern-challenges-fulvio-graziotto-wbrmf/

https://rsmus.com/services/family-office/family-office-rapid-assessment.html?dysig_tid=3b58324fffde425bb62ea34bc055fa9e#contact

https://quotefancy.com/quote/1220835/Marvin-Hagler-It-s-tough-to-get-out-of-bed-to-do-roadwork-at-5-am-when-you-ve-been

https://quotefancy.com/quote/768136/Arthur-Schopenhauer-Every-generation-no-matter-how-paltry-its-character-thinks-itself

https://www.octanner.com/global-culture-report/2021-generations

https://en.wikipedia.org/wiki/Generation_Z

Audiobook| Quantum mind: unveiling the secrets of consciousness

https://www.forbes.com/sites/russalanprince/2018/11/09/what-is-a-virtual-family-office/?sh=3125f95559d2

https://leverageedu.com/blog/rumi-quotes/

https://parade.com/1157722/michellehaag/running-quotes/

https://bernews.com/2024/03/minister-introduces-framework-for-family-offices/

https://f1experiences.com/blog/10-iconic-quotes-from-history-of-formula-1

https://www.marriage.com/advice/relationship/quotes-to-make-him-feel-special/

https://marriagekidsandmoney.com/generational-wealth-quotes/

https://timesofindia.indiatimes.com/blogs/the-photo-blog/remembering-gandhi-top-10-quotes-by-the-mahatma/

https://www.toptal.com/finance/startup-funding-consultants/fundraising-consultants-broker-

https://kpmg.com/us/en/capabilities-services/tax-services/international-tax-trade-and-transfer-pricing/international-tax.html

https://andsimple.co/insights/family-office-philanthropy/

https://jake-jorgovan.com/blog/family-office-consultants-consulting-firms

https://www.linkedin.com/pulse/risk-management-compliance-family-offices-fulvio-graziotto-zlxnf/

https://pubmed.ncbi.nlm.nih.gov/32906147/#:~:text=Results%3A%20Women%20experienced%20a%2045,losses%20associated%20with%20gray%20divorce.

https://www.investopedia.com/terms

https://www.goodreads.com/author/quotes/88582.Emmet_Fox

https://www.accaglobal.com/gb/en/student/exam-support-resources/professional-exams-study-resources/p4/technical-articles/islamic-finance---theory-and-practical-use-of-sukuk-

https://www.linkedin.com/pulse/family-offices-ethical-considerations-integrity-fulvio-graziotto-ythdf/?trk=article-ssr-frontend-pulse_more-articles_related-content-card

https://en.wikipedia.org/wiki/High-net-worth_individual

https://en.wikipedia.org/wiki/High-net-worth_individual#cite_note-worldwealthreport.com-20

https://familybusinessmagazine.com/family-education/family-governance-is-necessary-but-not-sufficient-for-transgenerational-success/

https://www.chinahighlights.com/travelguide/learning-chinese/chinese-sayings.htm

https://www.listofproverbs.com/source/c/chinese_proverb/112439.htm

https://www.rd.com/article/harry-potter-quotes/

https://familybusinessmagazine.com/family-education/family-governance-is-necessary-but-not-sufficient-for-transgenerational-success/

https://thefopro.com/the-new-billionaires/

https://www.afrasiabank.com/en/about/newsroom/africa-wealth-report-2021

https://grammigadvisory.com/

https://iqeq.foleon.com/brochure/multi-family-office/

https://www.agreusgroup.com/what-makes-the-perfect-family-office-legal-counsel/

https://dianachambers.com/

https://www.forbes.com/sites/krisputnamwalkerly/2024/03/07/plan-your-legacy-succession-in-family-foundations/?sh=2f0608f46571

https://www.journals.uchicago.edu/doiabs/10.1086/381475?journalCode=jpe

https://www-cnbc-com.cdn.ampproject.org/c/s/www.cnbc.com/amp/2024/03/08/family-offices-tripled-creating-a-new-gold-rush-on-wall-street.html

https://canadianfamilyoffices.com/fundamentals/whats-a-family-office-anyway-ten-domains-to-guide-them-all/wcm/aad9f9a7-5997-46b4-ac3b-d0de225e8f88/amp/

https://www.henleyglobal.com/publications/usa-wealth-report-2024/putting-people-first-and-behavioral-governance

https://andsimple.co/insights/masttro-family-offices/?utm_campaign=Insights&utm_content=286664517&utm_medium=social&utm_source=linkedin&hss_channel=lcp-10062499

https://emergiscap.com/the-latin-american-family-office

https://www.marshmma.com/us/insights/details/family-office-benchmarking-study/confirmation.html

https://womeninfamilybusiness.org/muna-al-gurg-innovation/

https://www.msn.com/en-za/news/other/15-most-powerful-and-richest-families-in-south-africa-in-2024/ar-BB1i3GFa

https://www.google.com/search?q=the+role+of+the+protector&rlz=1C1CHBD_enZA1067ZA1067&oq=the+role+of+the+protector&gs_

https://convergesolution.com/Adminimages/whitepaper/ConvergeSol%20Reporting%20Framework%20insight%20paper.pdf

https://www.legalandgeneral.com/insurance/over-50-life-insurance/later-life-planning/how-to-write-a-letter-of-wishes/

https://www.linkedin.com/pulse/estate-planning-people-blended-step-families-paul-hood-qrpqc/?utm_source=share&utm_medium=member_android&utm_campaign=share_via

https://www.linkedin.com/posts/tfoa_how-do-you-create-a-family-office-activity-7159184947155533824-zJ61/?utm_source=share&utm_medium=member_android

https://www.campdenfb.com/article/10-family-offices-owned-africa-s-wealthiest-people

https://www.ey.com/en_gl/industries/wealth-asset-management/five-priorities-for-winning-with-genai-in-wealth-and-asset-management?&utm_medium=email&_hsmi=300174947&_hsenc=p2ANqtz-_w_ziemH30BFK_WwYk7YXjcq-LJlyDc23d RxlAHJOfuFCErDuAHXYlFCZ5jsYv2CiDE5nOH9Mb6zphtNN8sVYc0y5haQ&utm_content=300174947&utm_source=hs_email

https://www.collascrilltrust.com/news-updates/articles/collectible-cars-investment-or-lifestyle-asset/

https://canadianfamilyoffices.com/commentary/macbeths-betrayal-three-financial-fraudsters-and-their-red-flags

https://dailyhodl.com/2024/03/31/1000-billionaires-begin-5200000000000-transfer-of-wealth-and-the-heirs-to-billionaires-have-their-own-ambitions-report/

https://www.nightingalehospital.co.uk/quotes-and-sayings-to-inspire-addiction-recovery-and-sobriety/

https://www.agreusgroup.com/how-are-family-offices-led-in-different-ways/

https://www.linkedin.com/business/learning/blog/top-skills-and-courses/most-in-demand-skills

https://www.linkedin.com/pulse/how-family-office-can-support-needs-robert-bobby-stover-jr-1eptc/?utm_source=share&utm_medium=member_android&utm_campaign=share_via

https://link.springer.com/article/10.1007/s11187-024-00907-1

https://www.linkedin.com/pulse/family-offices-investment-strategies-portfolio-fulvio-graziotto-zz3kf/?utm_source=share&utm_medium=member_android&utm_campaign=share_via

https://www.caproasia.com/2023/09/15/citi-global-family-office-insights-2023-268-single-family-offices-with-86-1st-2nd-generation-50-with-more-than-500-million-aum-top-3-concerns-are-inflation-interest-rate-increases-us-china-re/

https://www.vitreogroup.ca/vitreo-research/intergenerational-transfer-of-wealth-implications-for-philanthropy

https://www.thericciardigroup.com/global-wealth-report-thank-you-page/?submissionGuid=090973b2-e8ac-45b3-8436-888241f6a028

https://en.wikipedia.org/wiki/Astor_family

https://drsusanroets.com/

https://www.forbes.com/advisor/investing/how-to-invest-in-wine/

https://www.ey.com/en_lu/wealth-asset-management/the-future-of-family-offices--a-look-ahead-to-2024

https://fundcomb.com/lists/largest/family-offices/united-states-office

https://iqeq.com/insights/family-offices-in-asia-the-booming-powerhouses-of-asset-management/

www.famcap.com

The Four Agreements: A Practical Guide to Personal Freedom, book by Don Miguel Ruiz

https://www.climatechangenews.com/2024/04/19/global-billionaires-tax-to-fight-climate-change-and-hunger-rises-up-political-agenda/

https://dailyhodl.com/2024/03/31/1000-billionaires-begin-5200000000000-transfer-of-wealth-and-the-heirs-to-billionaires-have-their-own-ambitions-report/

https://www.oxfam.org/en/press-releases/less-8-cents-every-dollar-tax-revenue-collected-g20-countries-comes-taxes-wealth

https://www.southernliving.com/culture/family-quotes

https://www.monroecollege.edu/news/35-famous-accountants-surprise-inspire

https://www.taxadvisers.org.uk/historoftaxprofession/

https://en.wikipedia.org/wiki/Henley_%26_Partners

https://wealthx.com/reports/billionaire-census-2023

https://www.linkedin.com/pulse/5-reasons-number-size-family-offices-continues-grow-ronald-diamond-l6arc/?utm_source=share&utm_medium=member_android&utm_campaign=share_via

https://globallawexperts.com/lifestyle-management-and-concierge-services-of-family-offices/#~:text=Concierge%20services%20are%20specialized%20forms%20of%20lifestyle%20management,members%2C%20providing%20support%20in%20various%20tasks%20and%20activities.

https://www.forbes.com/sites/natalierobehmed/2014/07/14/the-vanderbilts-how-american-royalty-lost-their-crown-jewels/

https://www.tn.gov/commerce/securities/investors/what-is-a-security.html#~:text=The%20term%20%22security%22%20is%20defined,gas%20interests%2C%20and%20investment%20contracts.

https://www.pictet.com/hk/en/insights/psychology-of-wealth

https://www.businesstimes.com.sg/companies-markets/singapore-s-single-family-offices-likely-merge-find-alternative-models

https://www.agreusgroup.com/what-makes-the-perfect-family-office-legal-counsel/

https://www.dentons.com/en/insights/articles/2024/march/5/the-options-and-process-for-the-sale-of-a-family-business

https://www.linkedin.com/pulse/whats-difference-between-rich-wealthy-soumitri-das/

https://www.floridafunders.com/resources/blog/why-family-offices-are-investing-in-early-stage-tech/

https://www.pwc.com/gx/en/issues/c-suite-insights/nextgen.html?WT.mc_id=GMO-TRN-CS-FY24-INDF-NGS2024-T4-CI-XLOS-PUB-GMOTR00030-EN-OSLI-T7

https://clickup.com/blog/core-values-

https://scottjeffrey.com/core-values-list/

https://www.linkedin.com/pulse/family-office-investment-diversification-blue-chip-art-ty-murphy/

https://www.familywealthreport.com/article.php/New-Preqin-Report-Shows-Rise-In-Family-Offices

https://www.tharawat-magazine.com/stories/sustainability-long-term-value-family-businesses/

https://www.ey.com/en_gl/industries/wealth-asset-management/five-priorities-for-winning-with-genai-in-wealth-and-asset-management?&utm_medium=email&_hsmi=300174947&_hsenc=p2ANqtz-_w_ziemH30BFK_WwYk7YXjcq-LJlyDc23dRxlAHJOfuFCErDuAHXYlFCZ5jsYv2CiDE5nOH9Mb6zphtNN8sVYc0y5haQ&utm_content=300174947&utm_source=hs_email

Market study reveals more than 2,700 single-family Offices are thriving in Hong Kong | Deloitte China

https://www-technologyreview-com.cdn.ampproject.org/c/s/www.technologyreview.com/2024/03/18/1089899/how-ai-taught-cassie-the-two-legged-robot-to-run-and-jump/amp/

https://www.linkedin.com/pulse/how-handle-underperforming-family-employees-paolo-morosetti-wqwqf/?utm_source=share&utm_medium=member_android&utm_campaign=share_via

https://www.henleyglobal.com/publications/centi-millionaire-report-2023#:~:text=Notes%20and%20definitions,USD%20100%20million%20or%20more.

https://www.familyaddictionspecialist.com/blog/the-hidden-struggle-alcohol-addiction-and-substance-use-among-ultra-high-net-worth-individuals

https://www.morganstanley.com/ideas/private-credit-outlook-considerations?utm_content=287613097&utm_medium=social&utm_source=linkedin&hss_channel=lis-s5WWTvKC-W

Regenerative Visions For A Small Planet: Family Offices & Impact (forbes.com)

https://www.ubs.com/global/en/media/display-page-ndp/en-20231130-the-great-wealth-transfer.html

https://finance.yahoo.com/news/mark-cuban-predicts-worlds-first-181057110.html

https://medium.com/@jcgblue/are-you-rich-discover-your-ranking-in-the-global-wealth-report-7999591e183d

https://www.sarniayachts.com/family-office/

https://www.forbes.com/uk/advisor/investing/whisky-as-an-investment-all-you-need-to-know/

https://www.philanthropy.org.au/guidance-and-tools/ways-to-give/choosing-the-right-philanthropic-structure/

https://www.agreusgroup.com/the-role-of-culture-in-eastern-and-western-family-offices/

Singapore continues to tighten rules on Family Offices

Understanding the Impact of the Corporate Transparency Act on Your Family Office

The end of Non-Dom: What does this mean for Family Offices?

The paramount importance of selecting the right leader for your Family Office:
https://www.agreusgroup.com/who-is-the-ideal-family-office-leader/

https://karenkallie.com/discover-self-belief/

https://www.exotek.com/quote-of-the-week-11-08-2021/

https://www.srowlen.com/reliving-childhood-nostalgia-how-to-reconnect-with-your-past/

Take note

The book provides information on general principles. However, it's important to note that rules and regulations may vary depending on the jurisdiction. Therefore, seeking professional advice and support is crucial. Each matter is unique and has its own set of merits, and it's recommended to obtain specialist advice. Some of the information in the guidebook may differ from what you already know, so seeking formal advice is essential.

General disclaimer

All content is for informational purposes of a general nature only and does not address the circumstances of any individual or entity. Do not construe such information or material as legal, tax, investment, financial, professional, or any other advice. The content does not represent or constitute any solicitation, inducement, recommendation, endorsement, offer, or any third-party service provider to buy or sell securities, commodities, digital assets, or financial instruments. No information in the book constitutes professional and financial advice or a comprehensive or complete statement of the matters discussed.

Any information, materials, statements, and data set herein can change without notice. As such, no reliance must be placed on the fairness, accuracy, completeness, or correctness of any information and materials contained herein. You alone assume the sole responsibility of evaluating all merits and risks associated with using any information or material or coming to any conclusion based on the information and content found on the site.

There are risks associated with investing in securities, commodities, and property. Investing in securities and commodities such as stocks, bonds, exchange-traded funds, mutual funds, money market funds, and cryptocurrency involves the risk of loss.

The authors may provide hyperlinks to websites operated by and snapshots of the information supplied by or derived from third parties to inform you better. The authors have no control over such sites or content, so they will not assume any responsibility for such external sites' availability or content.

The authors do not adopt, endorse, or are responsible or liable for any such sites or content, including advertising, products, or other materials, on or made available through such third parties' sites or resources. The following information is provided for general informational purposes only and does not consider the circumstances of any individual or entity. Please do not interpret any information or material provided here as legal, tax, investment, financial,

One of the most beautiful qualities of true friendship is
to understand and to be understood.
Lucius Annaeus Seneca

In the generational landscape,
enthusiasm is our driving force.

anne Klein   *Brian DeLucia*

ABOUT THE AUTHORS

The authors of *Switching Billion-Dollar Conversation Lines, Family Offices & Multi-Generational Success* were introduced before the 2020 lockdowns.

Despite facing various professional, personal, and business barriers, they are keenly interested in family offices, founder-led companies, intergenerational planning, and creating opportunities for others.

Brian and Anne recognize that differences and challenges often lead to innovation and unity through *shared values*, leading to a greater purpose, similar to the history of successful families.

They created this book to share the knowledge and wisdom that they gained with the international family office community and the generational wealth profession — particularly in areas that are often a mystery to others.

Their single and shared experiences as well as their practical insights made it possible to author this useful and meaningful work.

To our Family, Friends, Industry Members, and the Families we serve ...

If you can give your child only one gift, let it be enthusiasm.

Bruce Barton

www.ingramcontent.com/pod-product-compliance
Lightning Source LLC
Chambersburg PA
CBHW061807210326
41599CB00034B/6913